The
Transformed
Lives
of Twenty-seven Contemporary Russians

Boris Mikhailov

The translation and publication of
The Transformed Lives
of
Twenty-seven Contemporary Russians
by
Boris Mikhailov

has been made possible by the people of God
at
First United Methodist Church,
Pensacola, Florida
U.S.A.

The Transformed Lives

of Twenty-seven Contemporary Russians

Boris Mikhailov

Russian Resources Press, Inc.
2001
1500 East Johnson Avenue Suite 123
Pensacola Florida 32514 U.S.A.
850 479 7962

Library of Congress Catalog Number 01 130141

ISBN 1-888676-09-4

Acknowledgments

We acknowledge our debt to each of the subjects of this book, who faithfully supplied the basic information from which the skilled writer, Boris Mikhailov, constructed this fascinating manuscript;

we offer gratitude to Sergei Nikolaev, Joun Soong Park, and Eduard Khegay for reading the early unedited text in Russian; to Pastor Oksana Petrova for invaluable assistance in contacts with author Boris Mikhailov in St. Petersburg, Russia; and to Dr. Elena Stepanova for invaluable assistance in clarifying many matters related to the manuscript;

we are grateful to Laura Arefieva Long, who with Troy and Rachel combined to give us an excellent translation from the Russian; to Pat Brinson, Lydia Istomina and Blanche Baskin, who carefully edited the English text;

and finally to Fran Jones and Evalyn Grubbs who served refreshing tea to the author and friends at the Hotel Pribaltiskiya on a sunny afternoon in St. Petersburg, Russia.

Contents

Publisher's Preface
to the English edition

Publishing Boris Mikhailov in English and Russian has been a delightful, if in some aspects taxing, experience. His manuscript came to me in Russian, so that was no problem. Getting the English translation into publishable form was more difficult, and I trust that we have not failed him in this regard. We have tried to maintain the integrity of the Russian idiom while moving the manuscript into a smooth read for those of us who don't have the ability to read the original.

I need to say, also, that spelling has been difficult. Whether to use Alexey or Alexei, Irina or Irena, or other combinations, seems to be a matter of personal preference. The Russians we have discussed this with differ. Some choose one, some the other.

On another matter. In working on this book I have become aware of the major role played by Koreans (both Korean-Russians and Korean-Americans) in the establishment and growth of the Russia United Methodist Church. Their ministries have been unique and fruitful.

I believe that this is an important book. It records the remarkable changes which have occurred in the lives of many Russians. We believe that the future of the Russian nation can be changed through the influence of these and other transformed lives.

George Baskin

Introduction

A note to the reader:

There are three things that I would like to say about this book before I begin the introduction.

First, I have included brief sketches of only twenty-seven of what I call "the transformed lives." There could have been thirty-two or fifty or even more. Many pastors of the Russia United Methodist Church should have been included. But the publisher reminds me that we have definite space limitation.

Second, the brief introduction I have included here does not even begin to tell the reader about the work of the United Methodist Church around the world. For instance, I have not often made mention of the Methodist Church in Germany, and the fact that Bishop Ruediger Minor, now our Bishop in Russia, was an active Bishop in the Methodist Church in East Germany before he was given his present responsibility. He is doing an incredible work in a remarkably difficult task.

And finally, a large part of this introduction tells about how I came to write this book, about what had happened in my own life before I began to believe that God wanted me to write the book.

BM

This book is about Methodists, followers of the teachings of Jesus Christ and John Wesley. For those who may not know anything about Methodism, I would like to explain how Methodism was born in England in the Eighteenth century. Its founders were the brothers Wesley, John (1703-1791) and Charles (1707-1788). Coming from a family of Anglican priests, John finished the School of Theology at Oxford University and then taught at the same school. In 1729

Charles formed a student club which was called derisively "The Holy Club" and "Methodists," of which his brother John became a member. Members of the Club believed and taught that members should live according to the Gospel. They tried to devote their time to prayers and good deeds. They helped the poor, preached to them, visited prisons and shelters for homeless people, and studied the Holy Scriptures. They did everything in an orderly and methodical manner, and that is why they were called "Method-"ists.

Charles, a few years younger than John, wrote about 6,500 hymns. Many are familiar, and one of the most beautiful of these is "Jesus, Lover of My Soul."

John traveled—on horseback, in coaches, or on foot—to the remotest corners of England, often sixty miles in a day, averaging four thousand miles a year for forty years. He preached and preached, bringing the Gospel of Jesus Christ to as many people as was humanly possible at a time when England was in desperate spiritual need.

John Wesley wrote the following about the church which had (although not by his intent) separated from The Church of England: "Methodism is a church which does not demand that its members have the same opinions or the same form of worshiping God, but that all members fear God and are righteous."

The brothers Wesley founded the Methodist movement (1729) at their university (Oxford) at a time when religion was not well looked-upon. The Church of England was at a low ebb. John denounced the rotten economics system, the corruption of English politics, the inhumanity of slavery, and the horrors of British jails. "What were the results of the Methodist preaching? In one generation religion, that which had seemed to be dying under Anglican domination, became a vibrant element in English life, subordinate only to politics and war. . . . If we judge greatness by influence John Wesley was, barring William Pitt, the greatest

Englishman of his times." (Durant, Will and Ariel. The Story of Civilization, Part IX. Simon and Schuster: New York, 1965). In the roughly two-hundred-and-fifty years that followed, Methodism spread around the world, achieving a membership of over eight million in the United States alone, with over twenty-five thousand churches.

The Documents of the Second All-Russia Conference of the Russia United Methodist Church, approved in May 1998, present the Credo, the basic beliefs of Russian Methodism.

"We believe in God, Creator of this world, and in Jesus Christ, Redeemer of God's creation. We believe in the Holy Spirit, through whom we receive the assurance of God's gifts. Our mission is evangelization. It is directed toward people who do not know the Good News about Christ and who live without Christian fellowship. Our task is to introduce Christ to other people, to teach those who found Him in faith, to strengthen the churches, and to form new groups of believers in places where God leads us within Russia and the Independent Republics. In this we want to serve only the church and its Lord.

"We respect the great history of spirituality and faith in Russia, the Orthodox culture. We do not try to lead people astray from national traditions, but want to build the life of Methodist churches in Russia on Biblical foundations, thereby contributing to the spiritual revival in other churches and in the society in general. The words of Jesus Christ from the Holy Gospel of Matthew (Matthew 28:19-20) give an explanation of the mission of our church, 'Go therefore and make disciples of all nations, baptizing them in the name of the Father and of the Son and of the Holy Spirit, and teaching them to obey everything that I have commanded you. And remember, I am with you always, to the end of the age. Amen.'"

As soon as I began searching out information about Methodism, I found that it would not be correct to say that Russians did not know anything about the teachings of John Wesley before the Methodists came to Russia. One of the first Russians who studied American Methodist churches was a writer and artist, P.P. Sviniyn, who worked for the Russian Ministry of Foreign Affairs. In 1815 he published a book, *Colorful Experiences of Travel in America*, many pages of which told about prayer meetings in the Methodist congregations in Philadelphia (p.54).

Early reports to Russians about Methodism were not always accurate. In 1876, after he visited the United States, journalist M. Trigo published an article in the St. Petersburg's magazine *Delo* which was titled "Religious Sects in America." He wrote: "In essence, the national religion of the United States is Methodism" (*Delo*, 1876, #5, p.115).

Famous revolutionary and journalist Petr Lavrov wrote about the followers of John Wesley in the magazine *Otechestvennye Zapiski* (P.D.Lavrov, "North American Sects," *Otechestvennye Zapiski*, 1968, #4, pp. 460-465).

Bishop Ioann Mitropolsky, while working in Alaska in 1870-1877, collected a substantial amount of material about the history of religion in the U.S.A. Later, he published five volumes of his works. The first two were dedicated to the history of the beginning of Methodism in England and its spreading in America (Ioann Mitropolsky, *From the History of the Religious Sects in America*, part I, 1876, pp.103-116).

In 1882, A.P. Lopukhin, a liturgist in the New York Russian Orthodox Church and a graduate from St. Petersburg Theological Academy, published a book *Life Overseas* that told about the Methodist services in great detail.

Published in 1896, *The Encyclopedic Dictionary* by F.A. Brokhaus and I.A. Efron had six pages of the nineteenth volume dedicated to the history of the beginning and development of the Methodist movement (pp.187-192).

So we see that Methodism was not entirely unknown in Russia prior to the twentieth century.

I became a Christian, a believer in Jesus Christ, through the ministry of a young Methodist pastor in Samara.

My wife, Ludmila, and I lived most of our lives as atheists. And raised our children to be the same. We were christened as young children, but for our safety, we were never told about this and learned of it much later. By the time of my vision, when I began work on this book, I was a five-year member of the Samara Methodist Church. It was the first Russian Methodist church revived without the help of foreign missionaries but by the Will of God and hard work of its pastor, Vladislav Spektorov.

Vladislav grew up in a typical Soviet family. Since childhood, he had spent every summer in Tallinn, Estonia. He had spent a great deal of time with Georg Lanberg, the pastor of the Estonian Methodist church. There he learned about Jesus Christ and the teachings of John Wesley. After study and prayer, he felt led by the Spirit to open a Methodist church in Samara, his native city on the Volga River.

He brought me, a communist and non-believer, to his church and helped me to repent and accept Christ. Of course, it did not happen in a night, not even in a year. I cannot really say the date when I realized that I could not live without an everyday relationship with God. It was a slow process of coming to God, which included Bible study, Bible School classes, and TV sermons by Dr. Robert Schuller, which I watched for almost five years. The years passed, but I still remember Dr. Schuller's sermons which I heard during my first days of being in the church: "Do not live without God. Go to the Orthodox Church! If there is no Orthodox Church nearby, go to Catholic, Protestant, Baptist, or any Christian church. But do not live without God. If there is no Christian church, go to the mosque, but do not live without God." These words changed something in my soul; they strengthened my faith.

As a youth, I listened to the radio stations from the West, so I had learned a great deal about the October Revolution of 1917. I knew about Stalin's camps and the Communist Party. While studying in the university, I used to read pirated copies of *Doctor Zhivago* and books by Alexander Solzhenitsyn. After school, though, I had to join the Communist Party to keep my job in journalism. I remained a journalist for almost 40 years of my life. Those years one could not be a professional without joining the Party. So, I dutifully obliged and paid my monthly fees.

Later, when I was coming closer and closer to God, I started to wonder if God would forgive my deceit. I knew the truth but still served the Anti-Christ. I gave myself the only excuse I had—the entire country lived the same way. We all said one thing, thought another, and did yet another.

Although during my whole career I have never intentionally or knowingly written or said anything untrue, I have committed no lesser sin. I sang praises to the things people in power wanted me to and kept silent about all the negatives. I kept silence about the repressions, the corruption of the Government, the made-up figures of the Five Year Plans, et cetera. That was the reason for my doubts, my fear that I could not be forgiven. I did not know that *if we confess our sins, he is faithful and just and will forgive our sins and purify us from all unrighteousness* (1 John 1:9).

In 1990, I quit the Party and decided to end my political involvement. I quit my job at the television news agency in Samara, where I had worked for over ten years. I was offered the opportunity to start a new international TV program without any political affiliation. It was a year of National Revival, with National and cultural centers opening across the nation. People wanted to know about their history and culture. I excitedly and gladly accepted the offer and launched the transmission of the TV show "We Are Russians." Many nationalities and peoples populated the Volga shores: Mordva, Chuvashes, Tatars, Bashkirs, and later Germans, Polish, and Jews. For many years, the Soviets were trying to make them forget their cultural and ethnic features, even their languages. They created a "new nation"—The Soviet.

At first, our new TV program showed different folk-groups and ensembles. Then, we started talking about cultural celebrations, including religions. Changes were happening rapidly in Samara, including the opening of the Lutheran Church and the Catholic Polish Cathedral. The Jews celebrated the rededication of their synagogue and the Orthodox of their churches. One could see the pastors and ksendz, rabbis and mullahs.

I have a very special memory regarding the Samara TV program, particularly the participation of Victor Ryagouzov, the elder of the Samara Baptist church. He was the first to teach a television Bible course. This took place even before the Russian Central TV began translation of Dr. Schuller's services. While making those programs, I learned a lot about God and Christianity.

On December 24, 1992 I was hosting a live broadcast from the Christmas celebration of the German Lutheran church when Vladislav Spektorov approached me. He introduced himself as a pastor of the Methodist Church and said that he and his parishioners were Russians and, as all Protestants do, celebrated Christmas the same day. Afterwards, they invited me to participate in their meetings. They did not have a church building and were renting one of the "Houses of Culture." I had never heard about Methodists before so I was very curious when my news team and I went to their church meeting. We produced a program about their Christmas celebration. In addition, we interviewed the pastor, who talked about Methodism and the new church in Samara. Two weeks later, the Methodist Church celebrated the Orthodox Christmas as well, and Vladislav invited me and my family to come. We all enjoyed the service, and especially liked the sermon. Also, the parishioners seemed to be very nice people. So, we decided to attend the next Sunday as well. My wife Ludmila and our son Lev, a student of the

Technical University at that time, and I, became members of the church.

My son was invited to come to the student group. He plays the guitar and very quickly became involved in the group's work. He invited his friends and soon evolved into one of the leaders of the group. Later, after his graduation from the university, with the recommendation of pastor Vladislav, Lev entered the Moscow Theological Seminary of the Russia United Methodist Church. During his second year of study, he and his seminary friend Valery Patkevich started a new Methodist group in Moscow. They called it "The Church of Saint Apostle Paul" and would go there to preach in their free time. In 1999, my son finished the Seminary and was appointed as a local pastor.

In April of 1997, because of the financial difficulties in the Samara TV station, my program "We Are Russians" was canceled, and I had to retire at the age of sixty-one. It was very hard for me to part with a beloved profession, but a far more serious trial lay just ahead. My wife became seriously ill. In spite of all our prayers and care from the fellowship, she did not get better. The Lord called her to be with Him.

I was very lonely. Often I would go to see Lev in Moscow, attend some of his classes at the Seminary, and go to the services of different Moscow Methodist churches. Then I would go back home to Samara, and try to earn a little money by writing articles for newspapers and magazines.

At that time I had my happy vision which led me to the writing of this manuscript. The idea of writing this book was given to me by the Holy Spirit. One night I was sitting in front of my typewriter struggling with an article I had been commissioned to do about a famous Russian professional stunt man. It was going slow; the right words would not come to mind. This was likely occurring because the person I was writing about did not interest me. Everything in me was protesting this story, but my professional duty demanded completion of the order.

After I had written a line or two, my eyes began to close and I kept sinking deep into thought. During one such moment I heard beautiful music. In front of my eyes I was seeing episodes from movies in which the hero of my article performed. Then suddenly something different happened. I began to see strange figures in white with washed-out silhouettes. My first impression was that I was seeing angels! However, something was bothering me. Why did their faces not look like those of nice creatures? Why did they not resemble the pictures decorating the walls of the Orthodox churches?

At that time the figures of the angels began to disappear into the darkness. In place of them I began to see the face of a bearded man with a light aura, a halo, around his head. Suddenly, I realized—it was The Lord Himself! I wanted to see Him closer, clearer! Unfortunately, His face seemed to be covered with half-transparent material, very thin and light, like that used to make women's scarves. All I could see was His gaze directed at me. The Apostle John wrote in his last letter, *No one has ever seen God* (1 John 4:12).

Then I heard a Voice behind my back, talking to me. I tried to turn around but my head did not want to move. It was as though somebody was holding it in place. The voice said, "Praying about salvation, but what do you do for the glory of The Lord?"

I tried to explain, telling Him that I pray every morning and night, go to church every Sunday, and follow the commandments. I was going to tell Him how differently I treated people now as well, but the Voice stopped me,

"Repent! You are too proud of yourself!"

This is from the Bible. I checked later.

"When you sit down at your typewriter, do you think about God? Did you write anything about My church?"

I tried to make an excuse saying, "No one would publish it!"

But the Voice did not let me finish, "They will. With My help."

And then the face of The Lord, or the One I saw, vanished and I noticed the piece of paper in the typewriter with the first lines of the article with which I was struggling. I rubbed my eyes and looked around. Was it all just a dream? It could not have been! I heard the Voice so clearly!

After my vision, I just could no longer delay beginning to work on the book I had been contemplating. I thought that there had not been even one book written about the revival of the Russian Methodist church by a Russian author. I did not know about Lydia Istomina's book *Bringing Hidden Things To Light.* It was translated into English and never published in Russia.

I had my vision late Saturday night. On Sunday, when I went to my church, I heard the news that Ruediger Minor, the Bishop of the Russia United Methodist Church, was visiting Samara and would be taking part in the worship service. It seemed to me like a continuation of my vision. I was looking forward to talking to him and asking his advice on the future book.

After the service, I introduced myself and told him of my vision. The Bishop approved my idea and we prayed together for the successful writing of my book. Shortly thereafter, I began to research the history of the Methodist Movement in Russia and collect material for publication. I went to the services of the churches I am describing in my book, visited with their leaders and parishioners. Then, I worked at different museums, including the library of the Russian Orthodox Theological Academy in St. Petersburg, and the State Archive of the former Capitol of the Russian Empire.

This book is fruits of my labor. God helped me to write it and present it for your judgment. Its heroes have taken, as I have, long and complex paths to the Lord.

I would like you to meet twenty-seven leaders of churches in the Eurasian Annual Conference of the Russia United Methodist Church on the next pages of my book. I wish I could have included every one of these wonderful men and women who have given their lives in service to the Master! Their lives have been truly transformed.

Boris Mikhailov
St. Petersburg, Russia
November 2000

The
Transformed
Lives
of Twenty-seven Contemporary Russians

Alexander Kaminin

And the prayer offered in faith will make
the sick person well.
James 5:15

In the late 1970's, Alexander Kaminin was a student at the Kuban Medical Institute in Krasnodar. A tall black girl from Liberia named Chris Hena was always noticeable among other foreign students in his class. While talking to Russians about almost anything she loved to tell them about God, Jesus Christ, and the Christian faith of Methodists.

Her stories were interesting, but in the Soviet times nobody believed in God or if they did they had to hide it. In 1982 Alexander finished his school and was sent to a small hospital in the village of Ilyok-Koshary in the Belgorod Region. He was put in charge of a small facility with one Physician Assistant on staff and ten empty beds. Patients came primarily to seek help after participation in drunken brawls.

Even though the building was in very bad repair and could not properly be called a hospital, the young doctor did not despair. Much of his time he dedicated to the building of a new hospital and to the search for good modern equipment. He was fortunate to have help from the Regional Office and the Collective Farm Administration in the village. In a few years, the village of Ilyok-Koshary had a nice new hospital with very good medical equipment. People learned about it very fast and soon patients from distant places began coming to see the Doctor. He even had to hire additional personnel to take care of all his patients.

Busy with medical and construction problems Alexander would have fast forgotten his black classmate if not for her letters from Africa. From time to time she would write to him, telling how she was staying busy not only treating patients but healing her tribesmen spiritually and preaching the Good News to them. Alexander felt sorry for her. Why would she study for six long years in a Medical school to only return to such primitive methods later?

More than ten years passed before Alexander saw Christina again, and by then she was back in Russia. She came as a representative of the General Board of the United Methodist Church and was responsible for a Medical Program in Russia. She came to Ilyok-Koshary and again told Alexander about God, and about the joy that he was missing in his life without Jesus. That time, the seeds of faith fell in moistened soil and began to grow. During all the years of his medical practice and the building of the hospital, Alexander became wiser and not once asked himself why medicines and operations helped one person and did not help another.

I started to think, and realized that if I sinned or acted against my inner voice and intuition, then the result was different from desirable. A person always knows when he acts from his heart and conscience and when he cheats and sins. We cannot fool ourselves. I began asking the Lord's help with my patients' problems, and they were often healed. I had a few patients who previously went to the Regional or City Hospitals and without getting better. Then, they came to my clinic and were healed! How can I explain it other than God's intervention?

Sometimes, I remembered arguing with Christina when she told me that in the United States some doctors use the

Word of God as a part of their main treatment. Then, I only laughed, "When a person had lost his arm, his doctors should pray and the arm would grow back in place?" Years later, I realized that a kind word, especially God's Word, played such a great role in the healing process. *The Lord will sustain him on his sickbed and restore him from his bed of illness* (Psalms 41:3).

In 1996, Christina invited Alexander to attend a conference dedicated to the role of the church in drug and alcohol addiction treatment. Leaders of the Russia United Methodist churches, psychologists, and psychiatrists came to Voronezh from many places. They shared their experiences of the work they started. Alexander was not doing any specific work with alcoholics yet, but he told the conference about the severe drinking problem in his village. Due to the lack of opportunity and low education many turn to alcohol, from ten-year-old boys to the oldest men. There was not a sober person in the village during holidays. People got into drunken fights and tractor "carridas," often killing and injuring each other. Fellowship with colleagues—doctors and other participants of the Conference, all of whom were Christians—made Alexander think. He remembered Christina's words about God because each day at the Conference began and ended with a prayer. Christina told the gathering about the experiences of the American churches that helped alcoholics and drug-users.

The last day was a service of Holy Communion, which was held by Bishop Minor. For the first time, Alexander shared in the body of Christ and His blood. He was deeply touched by Bishop Minor's words during the Communion and felt as if he were a part of something big and joyful.

I felt the presence of God and that day became my second birthday. All of a sudden, I realized that I had lived with Him for a long time but had not known it. I repented and accepted the Lord Jesus Christ with all my heart and never parted with Him again. Whatever I do, I always ask God's advice and His approval. I had been hesitating for a long time, but the Voronezh Conference, meeting with Methodists and having everyday prayers, helped me to find an answer to my questions.

Even before his life in Christ, Alexander always helped people. He chose to be a physician because of the opportunity to help. He often gave medicines to people who could not afford them. He always let elderly women from distant places stay overnight in the hospital and gave them free medications. Although he risked being reprimanded by the Medical Regional Office, he always did what the Holy Spirit told him.

Christina helped Alexander meet some American friends by correspondence and they sent a new computer for the hospital. The older one Alexander gave to the village children. Together, they remodeled one of the empty rooms in the village club (Community House) and Alexander began giving computer classes.

During breaks between classes, Alexander told children about Christ, read the Bible, and showed them videos about Jesus Christ, his apostles, and other Biblical heroes. As he learned the Good News, he was eager to share it with others. Children loved his lessons. Soon, American friends sent them a modem, so children were able to explore the Internet and to learn about the entire world.

Even while working with the kids, I always remembered my adult patients and preached to them the Word of God during my clinic hours and home-visits. For many, it became a new revelation. They loved to listen to my stories and ask questions. They say that they feel bad about not having a church in their village where they could go and pray. I explain to them that they can pray at home too, and that the Lord will hear them. They like the idea of talking directly to God as Methodism teaches.

In 1998, the Collective Farm administration gave Alexander a small piece of land where he and his followers have been building a church. Bishop Minor appointed Alexander as local pastor.

When the building is finished, there will be rooms for music group rehearsals and for the computer classes.

Every man should build something during his lifetime, so he could be remembered by it. I have already built a hospital with twenty staff members and twenty-five beds for patients. Now, I am building the Lord's church. I always felt the hand of God who supported me. Every minute I need His help.

The church congregation in Ilyok-Koshary is not big, about twenty children and six or seven adults. But they hope that when the church construction is finished, many more will join them. The most important part of his story is a witness that a Soviet Doctor, Alexander Kaminin, came to the Lord. He realized that medicine and faith should not be antagonists. One adds to the other. Spiritual treatment sometimes is more effective than any other medicine.

Elena Stepanova

She speaks with wisdom,
and faithful instruction is on her tongue.
Proverbs 31:26

Elena Alexeevna Stepanova is very well known in the Methodist world. The Lord has put many responsibilities on her shoulders. Just one of these duties would be enough for another person. But Elena has courageously undertaken this heavy load. She preaches at least once a week for the members of her church. She visits prisoners under her care. She carries out the duties of District Superintendent in the largest district in all of Methodism. One of her most important tasks is raising her two daughters, Masha and Dasha. Only God's help enables her to do all of her work. The Lord helps her a lot!

I had been thinking for a long time about my story regarding Elena and where it should begin. Finally, I decided upon the time when she first learned about Methodism and accepted it as her own faith.

Elena Stepanova remembers,

I have been interested in the history of world religions ever since I was in high school. It was then I learned a little about Methodism. My university diploma, and then my Master's thesis were written from the Marxist-Leninist point of view, a sign of the times. Of course, at that time I did not believe in any religion. Religion simply helped us to learn about the historic periods of humanity. My post-doctoral dissertation, defended in 1999, was dedicated to religious and philosophical matters.

Boris Mikhailov:

Very often a person comes to the Lord when he or she is older and has already acquired some of life's experiences and knowledge. Then, his/her philosophy on life has to be reviewed before a new decision is made. It involves refusing something and looking at other things from a different perspective. I know that you came to God as an older person and not in a moment. What was the beginning, what triggered it?

Elena Stepanova:

It began with the destruction of Communist ideals, with Gorbachev's perestroika and the wind of freedom. However, it was not linked to any ideology.

Actually, it all started with a June phone call from a teacher of the English language at the school that Elena's children attended. In spite of the fact that it was vacation time, the teacher invited children to come to school for a meeting with visiting American children. They would get to practice their English. Elena went along with her children because she wanted to talk to the older members of the American group. (A couple of months earlier she had returned from a business trip to the U.S. and still was full of memories.) The day after she took her children to meet the Americans friends invited Elena to come to the House of Friendship and Peace to meet all members of the American delegation. There, she met other Russians—Lydia Istomina and her sister as well as other friends and acquaintances. During the Soviet years the city of Ekaterinburg was closed to foreigners, so people were very excited about the first American group. The leader of the group was a Methodist pastor and preacher from Louisiana, the Rev. Dwight Ramsey.

Elena remembers,

> Curiosity brought me to the House of Peace and then to the university where Lydia Istomina had organized the meetings with Dwight Ramsey. I wanted to hear what he would say about his religion and to see the reaction of the audience. So it happened that Lydia, her sister Irina, myself, and many other young university professors as well as just curious people who had free time in summer, came to all the meetings with Ramsey. Lydia Istomina had asked Dwight Ramsey to help us start a Methodist Church. During one of the last meetings, he suddenly asked, "Why won't you start a church here, in your city?"
>
> Several said, "Why not? We can open a church!" The time was different, and everything seemed possible. Why do we need a church? I did not even have that question in my head. At the dawn of perestroika it was not too complicated. We had to collect twenty signatures of people who wanted to start their own organization. Lydia Istomina and Vladimir Tomakh, who later became a member of the church with his wife Tatyana, collected more than six hundred signatures in less than two months..

Lydia Istomina was elected Lay Leader of the first Methodist community in Russia in July, 1990. Soon, the first Russia United Methodist Church was registered after a seventy-year period when the Methodist Church in Russia was non-existent. The Americans stayed in Ekaterinburg for two weeks and then left, but the sparks of our interest towards God stayed. Eager for new knowledge and light, people kept meeting at the university for Bible Study. They read and discussed the Holy Scriptures.

Later, Elena remembered,

> I cannot truthfully say that Dwight Ramsey's sermons had a great influence on me. I had heard many different

sermons while in America. I was more curious about what would come of our meetings! I did not really think about God.

Many of Elena's colleagues did not care what kind of lectures they gave. They could lecture either for or against God. This attitude offended Elena. Those lectures were an extra job for her as well. But even during the Soviet times, she did not consider it important to prove the existence of God or His non-existence. She simply felt that He was created by a person's imagination. Her lectures titled "The Russian Orthodox Church, Its History and Present Day" were of an informative nature. Theology was her hobby and continuation of her scientific research was important to her. Elena liked to speak in front of an audience and explore her discoveries and theories. She was invited to give her lectures at many different places. Factories, Scientific Research facilities, schools, and universities were among them. She was touched by the naïve questions of her listeners. She told them the Biblical stories and explained the histories behind famous religious paintings. Several generations of Russian people grew up not knowing anything about the cultural world heritage which was so closely linked to religion. They saw religion as something dark, long dead and not intended for present time. Elena's lectures became revelations for some people. She was always very well-accepted.

When Elena was little, she found the New Testament in her grandmother's belongings and read it. She remembered it as a collection of amusing and unbelievable stories, but did not remember the name of the book. Elena became interested in world culture after she had an Ancient World History class in middle school.

After graduation from high school, she knew what she wanted to do. She entered the Journalism Department at the university. Later, when she became a teacher and was well-educated in world religions, she read many manuscripts while researching the Holy Scriptures, but not the Bible itself.

Only later, while visiting America in an exchange of scholars, was she able to hold the Bible in her hands and read it. She went as a part of an intern exchange program, which was dedicated to Russian religious philosophy. In America, she had a chance to get acquainted with the classic works of world philosophers which were not allowed in Soviet Russia. She visited the services of many Protestant churches. The prayer meetings left her with a strange impression. She was trying not to get involved emotionally, and to analyze everything from a scientist's perspective. She did not even think there could have been a seed of truth in the fact that so many intelligent and outstanding people in the world claim to be believers. Raised in the USSR, Elena refused any religion.

B.M.:

Did you know much about Methodism when you first met Dwight Ramsey?

E.S.:

I was just involved in religious matters. If somebody told me that those meetings would become a turning point in my life and bring me to God, and that one day, I would be a spiritual leader, I would have called that person a liar. However, after Ramsey left, my friends and I kept on gathering for prayer meetings and biblical discussions. At first, they were not prayer meetings, but simple get-togethers of friends. Even then I began asking myself why I kept coming there if I did not expect to receive any useful information for my work. I just kept feeling a strange calling to come. It was interesting, a different dimension of viewing life. We all had a great "dreaming" period. The number of people who came to our meetings kept increasing.

In the fall of the following year, another Methodist missionary group led by Bishops William Oden and Hans Vaxby (of the United

Methodist Church in the United States and the Northern European Conference, respectively) came to Ekaterinburg. The Philharmonic Auditorium was rented for two days. The group began their evangelization ministry. Both days the room was full. People were offered an opportunity to get baptized, and many wished to receive Holy baptism. People who had lived without God for so many years were eager to repent and receive Christ. The Bishops consecrated Lydia Istomina to be a local pastor.

Elena remembers,

Lydia had great organizational skills. She was able to talk the City Administration into letting us meet in one of the best buildings in the central part of the city—the Former Communist Propaganda Center. Lydia, as pastor of the church, was working on the congregational growth and development of the church along with the humanitarian projects for Russia, and I was asked to lead the Bible school and also the choir. We all were eager to work and showed a great deal of enthusiasm. About a hundred people came to our meetings, and they all did everything they could for the church. The average age of our members was thirty to forty years. They were teachers, doctors, engineers, and university professors. Most of their children came also. Lydia preached in our church almost every Sunday and also in the local prison. She also encouraged us, the lay members, to try. Sometimes I took over. Others tried as well. Everybody studied and learned.

After the official registration with the Government people began to treat these meetings more seriously. It was not 'get-togethers' any more, but real prayer meetings. The pastor used materials left by the missionaries to create the services. Elena helped, using her experience in the American churches she had visited. The choir combined from the young and not so young people enthusiastically learned the Methodist hymns. At first, they sang them in English, but later, found out that the Baptists had already translated many of them. So, they learned them in Russian as well. Choir practices united people and let them feel the unity of their souls and desires.

Elena says,

I was very surprised at myself. What happened that I got so involved in that strange way of life? But one day, I realized that I had a light in my life. Some different and new reason for living. It was as though I was a new person. My discovery was like an exploded bomb. This is how much I was shocked by my new life and new world.

I cannot really name a date of my turning to God. My long-acquired knowledge was slowly turning into new experiences. Some things happened without my noticing. All of a sudden, I started to realize that I began addressing God in my thoughts and that there was no way back. A strange transformation was happening to me, but I did not know whether I wanted it or not. For a long time, I did not ask myself if I had become a believer or not. I tried to avoid thinking about it. Sometimes I thought that I was just playing a game and my new life was not real. I thought that when I felt like I got too involved I would just quit. I agreed with St. John in his Gospel, *As for the person who hears my words but does not keep them I do not judge him. For I did not come to judge the world, but to save it* (John 12:47).

Dwight Ramsey became our church's supervisor. He came to Ekaterinburg quite a few times. During one of his visits, I was baptized. I was getting very involved in the life of the church fellowship and read many works of the philosophers all over again. The Bible became my desk book. Sometimes, I'd read it like just another reference and everything would be the same. But all of a sudden, I would feel such light coming upon me! *I have come into the world as a light, so that no one who believes in me should stay in darkness* (John 12:46).

Lydia Istomina encouraged me and Olga Kotsuba to think about joining the ministry as pastors. She shared this with Dwight Ramsey. When the Rev. Ramsey came to Ekaterinburg the next time, he asked Elena Stepanova and Olga Kotsuba to be local pastors. Some time passed. Lydia and Elena were in constant conflict.

Now, ten years later, they realize that all of their problems were in their own ambitions. Each tried to prove that she had the more important role. When they understood that God was the most important, the conflict was over.

But the church had already been separated into two different congregations. Lydia remained the pastor of one, and Elena headed another. Only after newly appointed Bishop Minor of the Russia Methodist Church recommended that they read a passage from Paul's First Letter to the Corinthians did the communities reconcile. Paul foresaw a similar situation and wrote, *I appeal to you, brothers, in the name of our Lord, Jesus Christ, that all of you agree with one another so that there may be no divisions among you and that you may be perfectly united in mind and thought* (1 Corinthians 1:10).

Fortunately the missionary ministry which the church was doing from the very first days did not stop because of the division. They distributed humanitarian assistance sent by the American sister churches, set up free meals for the poor, and continued visiting people in prisons.

Elena visited the prisoners on a regular basis. She finds her life meaning in visiting criminals and caring for their souls. She does not care as much about her university work any more. She feels very happy when she is able to tell others about Christ and salvation. She is very thankful when she sees the tears of repentance in the eyes of the prisoners. Elena made very good friends with some of them and can't wait to see them again. It was strange that there was so much in common between the accused criminals and the university professor. But in the first place, it was the Word of God. Elena remembers one of the encounters. A man whom she went to visit asked her skeptically, "Did you come to tease me? You have so much free time that you do not know what to do with it?"

Elena remembers,
> That person became one of the most attentive listeners. He was transferred to a different facility, but we still stay in touch through letters. I can see from them that our talks touched his soul. While visiting the prisoners I realized that those people who are so isolated in our society need God's Word the most. Our church has been preaching the Good News to prisoners for about seven years. The church members preach, deliver medications, collect clothes, and help prisoners to get in touch with their families. Often, they bring the prisoner's children from the orphanages to visit their incarcerated parents.

Now, Elena is an Elder of the Return to Christ Russia United Methodist Church and as District Superintendent of the Urals-Siberian District is responsible for oversight of fifteen other churches in the Urals and Siberia. She is a member of the Bishop's Cabinet, the Administrative Council of The Russia United Methodist Church in Moscow, and a Director of the General Board of Higher Education and Ministry. Also, she has earned the Doctor of Philosophy degree and is a professor at the Ural Technical University.

She is doing some translation work in addition to this. For example, she translated a part of The Book of Discipline of the United Methodist Church into Russian. She writes articles about Russia's Methodist Revival in English for publication in America.

Elena says about herself,

      Sometimes, it feels like a certain turn in your life was an accident, but later, you realize that it was not. I fully understood the words of my favorite Russian philosopher, Ivan Ilyin. He said that when a person walks on the path of faith, his whole life gets lighter and changes completely. The person finds his happiness in the Lord's service.

Dmitry Lee

I know that you can do all things.

Job 42:2

In some respects Dmitry Lee's story is much like that of thousands of other Koreans whose families have lived in the Russian Far East for centuries. In 1937 the Bolsheviks deported them to Middle Asia, and after Stalin's death they were scattered throughout Russia.

Dmitry was born in a small town not far from the city of Kzyl-Orda in Kazakhstan, his family somewhat more fortunate than others. Dmitry's parents, both teachers and specialists in the Korean language, found very good jobs in Kazakhstan. After the great Patriotic War in 1943 they were invited to work in Moscow. In 1954, the American-Korean War ended, and Dmitry's family, among many other Soviet professionals of Korean heritage, was sent by Stalin to North Korea to help Kim Il Sung build socialism.

So Dmitry happened to spend a few of his school years in the land of his ancestors in Pyongyang. Going to the only Russian school, he made friends with people whom he would meet again years later in Moscow. Their friendships would last for a lifetime: Tesei Yugai, Galina Tyan, and Valery Khae. They all would eventually come to the Methodist Church. His final year—tenth grade—Dmitry finished in Moscow. From here he was called to serve in the Army.

After service, he entered the Military Engineering Academy and decided to make his career in the military. He was sent to a surface-to-air missile defense garrison in the distant northern area. Dmitry was hoping to stay there for only a short time. He was receiving promotions and growing in rank, but his military speciality kept Dmitry isolated, far from larger cities. He did not even dream of returning to Moscow, but at least was hoping for a better place of service. All the long years of his service happened to be in sparsely populated areas, where life had to center around the military. One could not find anybody to talk to other than military personnel of the base.

The years passed. He had plenty of time to think about the reason for his life and human destiny. He considered these matters often. He was interested in questions of faith: why do some people believe in Jesus Christ while others believe in Buddha, yet others in Allah, and yet others in somebody or something else. The political Commander of the Garrison was supposed to help with ideological questions, to keep up the morale of his soldiers. But Dmitry was not satisfied with the answers because all his Commander could advise him was to seek the truth in a bottle of vodka.

Dmitry remembered,

I was longing for an intelligent, thoughtful companion to talk to; for a teacher who could help me search myself. My friends found their answers at the bottom of vodka bottles. My Korean roots and the way I was raised did not let me drink. Most of my time I spent with books. One of the books I remember was *The Bible for Believers and Non-believers* written by Emelyan Yaroslavsky. An atheist fanatic, Yaroslavsky took different Biblical stories and parables, quoted them and then criticized them from the materialistic point of view. I never liked propaganda and could always recognize it. But in that book I read the quotes from the Holy Scriptures. Instead of pulling me toward atheism, the book awoke in me deep interest toward God and the Bible.

After twenty-five years in the Army, Dmitry retired from the service and came back to Moscow. Family problems, the search for a new job and new friends took precedence over his doubts and search for God. But God did not fail him, and brought him to church.

Dmitry Enbarovich remembered,
  I came to church for the first time by chance. In the early 1990's with the beginning of perestroika the economic system in Russia was shaken. I was working as a lead engineer in a scientific facility and had a very good salary. But with each day the situation was changing; prices were going up and we started to feel the lack of assets. I felt I should look for a second job. I decided to talk to one of my good friends, Tesei Sergeevich, who had just started a new job as Korean translator for the new Protestant church. Tesei's family also had been deported from the Far East. He was working at the new Russian-American-Korean church where he made many friends with the Korean Moscovites and South Korean businessmen.

One of them was planning to open a new Tourist Agency, and Dmitry was hoping to get a job with the help of his friend Tesei Yugai. Dmitry came to the church to meet with his prospective employer. Waiting for the talk, Dmitry went to the worship service and learned that a free course in Korean was offered every morning before the service.

  We all grew up in a Russian environment and went to Russian schools. Sometimes, my parents spoke Korean to me at home, but although I could understand them, I always replied in Russian. So, I was happy to have the opportunity to study my native language.

At the same time, Dmitry accidentally happened upon a small book which reminded him of the atheistic Bible commentary by Yaroslavsky. From the book Dmitry learned that before his death, Yaroslavsky made peace with God. Not only that, but in his Last Will he asked that all of his books about atheism be burned. Dmitry was shocked by that new knowledge. Furious non-believer . . . Lenin's assistant in the destruction of religions and churches . . . Yaroslavsky repented?

Along with many other Russian Koreans, Dmitry began to stay for the worship service following the language class. At first, his main reason for this was fellowship with other Koreans. Later, the Word of God began its work in his heart. Prayers and the sermons touched the soul of the atheist. He started to feel the presence of the Lord in his daily life.

Pastor Cho Young Cheul did not hurry or push, but wisely strengthened Dmitry's newfound faith. It took a while for him to come to God, but one day he just realized that this was his future. He learned that one-third of all his fellow Koreans were Christians. It helped to shape his chosen path. Along with his new friends—Valery Khae, Vyacheslav Kim, Andrey Kim, and others—Dmitry entered the newly opened Theological Seminary of Cheul. Right before joining, he repented and accepted Christ.

I understand the power of prayer. *Therefore I tell you, whatever you ask for in prayer, believe that you have received it, and it will be yours* (Mark 11:24). And it is true. God grants all I ask Him for. God leads me in my life. I am not worried about material things anymore. I do not think about tomorrow because I am certain that the Lord will not leave me. And I received a new desire to share my new life with other people, to tell them how happy I am with the Lord. Listening to Cheul's sermons and talking to him, the fire began to burn in me and I wanted to bring the Good News to people and ask them to repent and accept the Lord.

Dmitry became pastor of the first Methodist church in Vnukovo, a suburb of Moscow. He helped to touch the lives of a small group of people with the Word of God. They were his first church members. Today, there are more than fifty regular parishioners. Dmitry's church produced other leaders, including Svetlana Alexeeva, Valentina Birukova, Natalia Shulgina (who is President of the Youth-Student Council of the Russia United Methodist Church) and many others. Leading by his own example of being a good Christian, he strengthened the faith of his followers and has brought to God tens of hundreds of brothers and sisters in Christ.

For a long time, the church did not have a building and was renting a hall in Aeroflot's House of Culture. In 1998, they were able to purchase a building that has since been remodeled into a church. Now they have rooms for prayer meetings, youth and children's group activities, and choir rehearsals. Also, the church was able to broaden its missionary work among the local population of Vnukovo.

As a result of Dmitry's role in the establishment of other Moscow churches and his active participation in the Administrative Council of the Russia United Methodist Church, he was elected Superintendent of the Moscow District.

Dmitry has found the answers for questions with which he had been struggling for many years, namely, why he was born and what his mission in life is. He now knows that he was born to serve the Lord and his mission in life is to live out his personal salvation, and to bring others, in need of salvation, to God.

Lydia Mikhailova

A good name is more desirable than great riches;
to be esteemed is better than silver and gold.
Proverbs 22:1

The conference room at the Moscow Intourist Hotel could not hold all who wanted to meet the visitors from America—the missionaries, theologians, pastors, and just plain people who were interested in Russia.

A short woman, future pastor but for now a student of the Theological Seminary of the Russia United Methodist Church, Lydia Mikhailova was standing at the pulpit. She had been asked to give a Christian witness to the crowd, and she seemed very nervous. There were not only seminarians in the room but also Bishop Ruediger Minor of the Russia United Methodist Church; Dmitry Lee, a pastor in Moscow and Superintendent of the Moscow District; church representatives; and most importantly, American guests. She was worried whether they would like and accept her. For her presentation, she had prepared a story about her life as her seminary professors had recommended.

After giving praise to the Lord, Sister Lydia began with stories about her mother and a statement about the importance of kind deeds. During Kruschev's "reign" her family had finally received approval to come home after their thirty-year exile in the Archangel region. So at eighteen Lydia had been transported to the southern region of Russia, standing on the land of her ancestors for the first time. She was discovering that life could be very different from the cold northern region. There were white houses with beautiful orchards and maple trees. For the first time, Lydia saw a very nice and solid brick house, built by her grandfather, from where his family was exiled to the distant Archangel Region in the 1930's.

She had already met people whose names she remembered from her Mother's stories, told to her during the long northern nights. Just a few days before several old women resting by the river had stopped her as she walked about this new and exciting land and asked, "Whose are you?"

"You won't know me. We just came back form the North."

"Is your mother's name Nadya (Nadezhda)?"

"Yes, but why?"

One of the women suddenly pulled Lydia toward herself and started to kiss her hands.

"Grandmother (a term of respect, not relationship), what are you doing?" Lydia was really surprised.

"I remember your family. I am eternally thankful to God for your grandfather. He saved our family from starvation in 1922. All of his wheat he gave to people. If not for him, half of our village would have died. We will never forget how he helped us to survive."

Another old woman added, "Your grandfather Moesey was very kind and hard-working. He loved his family so! Did your Mother tell you? When they came after you, they sent all of the family to the North, but he was sent to Kazakhstan alone. He died there within a year from loneliness. I remember we received a letter from a doctor, who was from here. He wrote that Moesey died although his body was absolutely healthy. He just could not survive being parted from his family."

"My mother never told me that! My parents never even told me that our family had been sent from here into exile. I learned about it only a year ago. So many years passed, but you still remember my Grandfather! How wonderful!"

With that story, Lydia began her sermon about the good deeds that are never forgotten. The kind eyes of Bishop Minor, her fellow students, teachers, and American pastors supported her and she stopped being nervous. The audience was listening very attentively.

Lydia's mother and father came from a traditionally large Cossack family. Her father had seventeen brothers and sisters; her mother was one of sixteen children. From early childhood, they were taught to work. How else could they provide for so many? They had to feed all of them, and buy them clothing. When the time came for one of the boys to serve in the army, his family had to provide a horse, ammunition, and a uniform. But the Red Army came and started to exile family after family. If you had a good house and cattle, it meant that you were rich, and therefore, bad, and had to be exiled at once.

Lydia's mother, Nadezhda, was a nineteen-year-old newlywed when the terrible process began. Her family and the family of her husband were taken away from their homes, put into a cold cargo train, and sent to the North. They were "dumped" in an isolated area in the forest, where snow was chest-high and there was no settlement for many kilometers. It was twenty-four miles to the nearest village and several hundred to the city of Archangel. The men immediately began to cut down some pine trees and built a big hut where fifty or sixty people could stay overnight. During the day, it was warmer but at night it was still below zero (Centigrade) even though it was March. Children and the weak began to die in the first few days.

When summer came, one-third of the settlers had died. They had to work as lumberjacks. The soldiers took them to the forest at six o'clock in the morning while it was still dark and brought them back at about midnight. Escape was impossible. Armed guards watched over them. Swamps surrounded the camp. If someone could escape, the locals would have never helped and would have brought them back to the camp. The local population was told that they, the "settlers," were "enemies of the people," bad criminals who had tried to starve Soviet people. So, the locals would not even give them a cup of water.

Lydia's mother was made a "pusher." When men cut the huge pine trees and fur trees, she was supposed to push it in the right direction to fall. When she became pregnant, only after her labor began was she relieved from work. They made her go back to the forest on the third day after her daughter's birth. Her first child, Lydia's sister Yulia, was a sickly baby. Everybody felt sorry for the baby because they knew that she had very little chance to survive such conditions.

Secret prayer helped them to bear with inhumane conditions. They could not even pray openly, because somebody could tell the KGB who would put them into prison and send them to another camp to do even more difficult work.

Time passed. Still in the camp, Nadezhda gave birth to two boys and three girls. The last one, Lydia, was born in 1948. Nothing changed in their lives. Every morning, they were escorted into the forest and brought back by midnight. One time, a daughter became ill and was fading right in front of their eyes. They needed to take her to see the doctor. Nadezhda asked the Commander to let her take the baby to the hospital in the town, located about twenty-four miles away. The Commander refused. But the baby became even sicker. Nadezhda tied her up with a towel to her back and went to the Commander's house. She told him, "I am going to leave even if you will not let me. Do whatever you want but I need to take her to the doctor."

The Commander yelled, "I am going to shoot you! Go back to your barracks, she will be OK! If not, you have five more! Just give her some herbal medicine."

Nadezhda did not have any choice. She wanted to save her baby, so she relied on God, turned around and started towards the road that would lead her to town. She heard two shots. She did not know whether he missed her or shot in the air. Later, she was told that the Commander's wife, also a mother, saved her. She pushed his arm and did not let him aim. The Commander brutally beat his wife.

When Nadezhda came back, he promised that she would pay for her disobedience later, but he never punished her. Lydia survived mainly because her heroic mother nursed her until she was two years old. It is still a mystery, how an always-starving woman could have some milk. Once when rations were very scarce she had to divide a piece of bread between all members of her family and then she divided hers between the children.

When Stalin died in 1953 they were allowed to work without constant armed guards. Nadya's children were allowed to go to the town's boarding school. Being the youngest, Lydia did not know much about her parents' past and their problems. Even when she finished high school, she still did not know that her family was "repressed" and sent to live in that distant northern forest against their will. Her parents protected her from that knowledge, which could only harm her.

The revelation came unexpectedly from the younger brother. A naïve young man, he wanted to enter the Institute of International Relations. When a well-fed bureaucrat returned his papers, he scolded, "Lumberjacks' kids do not study here."

The young man replied, "Whose children do?"

"Diplomats' children."

The young and naïve man from the northern province where his family lived in exile was so angry that he just had to share it with his sister Lydia. His sister was shocked even more. She was raised in the Soviet school and believed in fairness. She thought that all "rich" people were evil, and nobody was "repressed" without cause. Now, she was told that all of her uncles and her mother and father were enemies of their own people. For the first time, she doubted the Soviet ideology and way of life.

After reading Solzhenitsyn's *One Day In the Life of Ivan Denisovich* she did not believe what the great author had written. So she asked her Uncle Kostya, who was in the Solikamsk GULAG, if the book was truthful.

Her uncle did not know how to put it. "He wrote only one tenth of the truth! It was much, much worse. You know why I was put there? I refused to write an accusatory letter on an innocent man. Our local KGB agent was going to dictate to me what to write. Next day, four other people wrote similar papers on me, that I was not trustworthy and that I did not believe in victory over the Fascists. I was convicted and sentenced to ten years of hard labor."

As all others in the Children's Home, Lydia was a member of the Young Pioneers, and later of Comsomol. She had believed that the best way of life in the world was in her country. Now that idealistic world of her childhood was being shattered. She began to realize that life was not the same as they taught her or showed on films. She did not know anything about God. Her mother mentioned His name sometimes, but not more than that.

Lydia turned to God for the first time while she was a student at the university. She was going to the city of Norilsk with her fellow students when their plane caught on fire right in the air. That was when she remembered God. She began praying, "Lord, please! Help the pilots land the plane! Do not let us burn alive!" Whether by the skills of the pilots or God's help, the plane landed. After that time, though, Lydia did not think about God for a long time.

Later, the time came to give birth to her first child. Her delivery was difficult but she does not remember whether she asked for God's help in her labor pains. But when they brought her son for his first feeding, she exclaimed, "Lord, thank you for your gift!" Then, again came the chaos of life. Her job, her home and then another son did not leave a place in her heart for the Lord.

In 1988, during the days of celebration of the One Thousand-year anniversary of Russian Christianity, her sister in Kiev was able to purchase Bibles for herself and for Lydia. To read, and even more, to possess the Holy Scriptures was a forbidden dream. But as in all forbidden things, the book seemed to be very attractive. So, Lydia eagerly began reading it. However, without a kind teacher, she did not get past the family trees in the Old Testament. In a week, her interest in the Holy Bible went away, and she replaced it with her regular household chores and problems.

However, her husband Nickolay read it, and the Bible seemed to awaken something in his soul. He began attending the Orthodox church and enthusiastically dedicated himself to the church's mission work and helping others. It was as if he knew God would soon be judging his life.

Not far from Lytkarino where the Mikhailovs lived there was a church building which had been taken by the government and partially destroyed during Soviet times. This building had been recently returned to the Orthodox Church by the local authorities. Nickolay Ivanovich began helping Father Alexey to restore it.

As the vice-director of a Construction Institute, he was able to help get metal and building materials. He himself came and worked at the construction site. Father Alexey asked Nickolay Ivanovich to be baptized, but he answered that he was not yet ready. He said, "Let's restore the church and begin services. I will get baptized then." However, the Lord's will was different. Lydia's husband became seriously ill and was baptized in a hospital ward. Then, he confessed to his wife, "I did something wrong in my life that the Lord is punishing me for."

Lydia could not believe him. "You have always loved people, you never betrayed anybody and never stole anything. You are loved by everybody! Why do we have to go through this trial?"

The illness was terminal, and the Lord took Nickolay Ivanovich. For a long time, Lydia grieved the loss of her beloved husband and the father of her two sons. Her inner voice told her it was the will of the Lord, and that she should repent and turn to God. She obeyed it and began attending the Orthodox Church. Sometimes, her grief went away or hid deeper in her heart, but she could not find a complete peace.

One day a group of Americans from the sister city of Chickasha, Oklahoma, came to visit Lytkarino. The businessmen and professionals in the areas of culture, medicine, education, and religion wanted to establish initial contacts with the Russians. Lydia's friend talked her into inviting one of the American women to stay with her. A friend hoped that taking care of a guest would help Lydia forget her grief, at least for some time. That was how Lydia met the seventy-four-year-old Ruth King, who happened to be a missionary (a lay person) from the Methodist church. Ruth's first question was "Are you a Christian?"

"No, I believed in a higher being, but God took my husband and father of my children."

As a true Christian, Ruth was shocked by this answer. She began to assure Lydia that God knows better how to conduct the life of each person and it should not be viewed as punishment. When they sat at the table, Ruth said a prayer before eating her meal. The words of it were simple and clear, "Thank you, Lord, for this day and for letting me meet Russian people. Thank you for the roof over my head and our food. Bless this house, this food and the hands that prepared it!" It was so different, and deeply touched Lydia's soul.

Ruth stayed with her for ten days. Together, they visited local hospitals and child-care facilities, and listened to the sermons of the visiting pastor. In the evenings, they had long talks about God and the Methodist Church. Before leaving, Ruth made Lydia promise her that she would attend church. That American lady turned Lydia's life upside down. Lydia started to attend the Lytkarino Methodist Church.

Today if she is asked how she came to God, she says that it happened through listening to sermons and fellowship with other believers. Some time has passed, and she cannot imagine her life without God, a prayer, everyday reading of the Bible, and Sunday worship service. When the Theological Seminary of the Russia United Methodist Church was opened in Moscow, Lydia thanked the Lord and with great joy accepted her pastor and Bishop Minor's invitation to enter it.

This story, a testimony of her own life, Lydia shared in her sermon. After she finished, she heard a roar of applause. They never said a word that she had taken much more time than she was supposed to for her sermon. Her story greatly impressed the friends from America. The theologians noted her skills in writing a wonderful sermon and her talent in bringing it to the audience.

Several years have passed since that meeting. For a long time, Lydia has been serving as a pastor for the *Perovo Russia United Methodist Church*. It has over fifty members, and their number is increasing. In her sermons, Lydia uses her rich life experience and her encounters with different people to serve as illustrations to the teachings of our Lord Jesus Christ, the four Gospels, and the Letters of the Saint Apostles.

Nickolay Dalakyan

Praise be to the Lord, to God our Savior,
who daily bears our burdens.
Our God is a God who saves.
Psalms 68:19,20

Nickolay had to endure many trials before he repented and came to God. His father Genrikh was a talented engineer, but he left the family when Nickolay was two years old because he could not stand having a handicapped daughter, Aleena. Nickolay's mother was left to raise both children by herself and take care of Aleena. From time to time, she would go to the Orthodox Church to light a candle and to cry in front of the icon of Saint Mary with the infant Jesus. Not knowing the wisdom of God, she would ask the Divine only one silent question, "Why me?" Only many years later did she come to know the living God who had already answered her question in this manner, *Neither this man nor his parents sinned, but this happened so that the work of God might be displayed in his life* (John 9:3).

During Nickolay's childhood in Baku, Azerbaijan, the Lord was leading the family through the valley of trials. His mother got seriously ill and had to stay in the hospital for months. Nickolay went to live with his aunt. His father took Aleena to live with him at the other end of the country. God gave his father, who was looking for an easy life, a very hard load. However, the reward was great, as well. His family was going to be the source of salvation for many. But before this time would come, they had to pass through fire.

Genrikh was the Secretary of the local party organization. Young and handsome, he was always at the center of women's attention. But they lost their interest in him as soon as they learned about his invalid daughter. But a few years later he met a woman who was to become a second mother to Aleena, to share all their problems and sad times. They went to the best hospitals in the country looking for a cure, but their attempts seemed to be hopeless. It was hard to buy the expensive medications without which the girl had very severe attacks of the disease that threatened her life. But God's plan was already in action. In one of the Ukrainian hospitals, Aleena's roommate was a girl who was being cared for by her grandmother, a devoted Baptist Christian. Even though some of the children were mentally retarded, she still told them about Jesus and the Gospel. There in the hospital room Aleena repented in front of the Lord. That is when the Holy Spirit started its work in her's and Nickolay's family.

At home, Aleena refused to take her medications. Neither talks nor reminders about awful attacks that she previously had would change her mind. "Jesus Christ is my doctor," she would say. "He has the power and the way to heal me." Her parents could not do anything but wait, taking turns by the phone, expecting to have to call for an ambulance at any moment.

But they would never have to call for it again! *When he heard this, Jesus said, "This sickness will not end in death. No, it is for God's glory so that God's Son may be glorified through it* (John 11:4). However, this sign did not change her parents. For a few more years, Aleena kept praying and asking her parents to repent.

And then one day the neighbor invited Genrikh's wife, Ludmila, to come to the worship service at the local Baptist church. Aleena's prayers were answered! After a sermon from the pastor,

Ludmila was deeply touched, and she repented and gave her heart to Jesus.

Their neighbor went straight home and shouted in front of the apartment building, "Gena! Gena! Luda repented today!" (Gena is a nickname for Genrikh, Luda for Ludmila). Genrikh had no idea what repentance was, but he understood it was a reason for celebration. He ran to the grocery store and bought a special bottle of Armenian Cognac.

When happy Ludmila came to the door, he said, "Congratulations! People said that you repented. I do not know why but I do feel that we should celebrate!"

"No, my dear! I do not want to drink alcohol ever again in my life!" She was very happy and overwhelmed by emotions and wanted to share the joy from her fellowship with God.

Genrikh only laughed, not understanding his wife, "Only uneducated, retarded people believe in God. How can you take seriously all that nonsense?"

But now two people in the family were praying, Aleena and Luda. After a few visits to church, Nickolay's father opened his heart to Jesus. Right away, he wrote a letter to the Communist Party, asking to resign. He began witnessing to his colleagues. During Brezhnev's times it was unbelievable that the leader of the local Party Organization would quit for religious reasons. That could lead to KGB interrogations, treatment in a psychiatric ward or even assignment to a labor camp.

In the Party, Genrikh was really liked by his superiors, so his letter did not go far. They just dismissed him for not paying his membership dues! But the KGB still learned about him and asked him to come to their office. They shamed him and threatened, "How could you, the leader of the Party, an educated person and our leading engineer, get caught by the religious fanatics?"

Genrikh knew by then what Christ taught, *But before all this they will lay their hands on you and persecute you, delivering you up to the synagogues and prisons, and you will be brought before kings and governors for my names's sake. This will be a time for you to bear testimony. Settle it therefore in your minds, not to meditate beforehand how to answer; for I will give you a mouth and wisdom, which none of your adversaries will be able to withstand or contradict* (Luke 21:12-15).

He answered wonderfully, "There are three hundred people in our church who live righteous family lives. They do not steal. They work "as for the Lord." They do not drink. They do not even smoke. Tell me about another organization like this and I will join it!"

The KGB people could not say anything in response and they just tried to frighten him.

The whole family began to pray for Nickolay and his mother. And, of course, Aleena was praying the most. As soon as possible, Genrikh went to his native town (Baku) to talk to his son and to tell him about the salvation of Jesus Christ. But history repeated itself. Nickolay, who was a student at the Military Boys School and a member of Komsomol (Communist Youth Union), was shocked to hear about Jesus from his father. And if he did not laugh in his face, it was only because of respect for his father. He certainly felt pity for him. Nickolay was fifteen years old then. Genrikh sadly left his son. When they parted, neither knew that it would be a long sixteen years before they saw each other again. Nickolay would be thirty-one years old.

Many things happened to both families during that time. Genrikh's family actively preached the Gospel. Their church sent them to minister to Russians in the United States in the mid-1980's. Nickolay's repentance was always one of their main prayer requests. Nickolay himself entered the Mozhaisky Military Engineering Academy in St. Petersburg. But after about two years of studies, he realized that military service was not for him, and decided to go back to Baku, in Azerbaijan, to study at the Polytechnical Institute there. But first he had to complete the remaining time left on his two years of required military service.

When he finally got back home to Baku, his arrival coincided with the beginning of an international conflict (Armenia, mostly Christian vs. Azerbaijan, mostly Muslim). The Muslims were killing and exiling Armenians from their land.

So Nickolay and his mother had to leave Azerbaijan and went to Armenia as refugees in 1988. But the path of trials had not ended for them yet. They did not even have time to settle in their new place when a huge earthquake shook the town, killing many people and injuring others.

All these events led Nickolay to think about the reason of life. He started to look for truth. Studying in the daytime and working at night, he started to learn about different religions and philosophies, including Buddhism and Krishnaism. He read the works of Nietzsche, Schopenhauer, and Freud. He even read the Koran. With great difficulty he got a Bible, paying for it with his monthly student scholarship. It was a big disappointment. He did not understand anything. He learned later that it was easy to study and understand religions and philosophies because they all were created by other people. But the Bible was written under the guidance of the Holy Spirit and a person could understand it only with the help of the Spirit. *But the Counselor, the Holy Spirit, whom the Father will send in my name, will teach you all things and will remind you of everything I have said to you* (John 14:26). Nickolay finished the Institute, and led by his then favorite philosopher Nietzsche, tried to accumulate as much money as possible.

But the trials continued. His mother was diagnosed with cancer, and she needed to undergo treatments in Moscow. They had some relatives there who helped to put her into a Moscow hospital and helped Nickolay to start his own business. He worked during the day and took care of his mother at night. He did not have any energy or time left to continue his search for the reason of life.

But far away, overseas, his family kept praying for Nickolay's salvation, despite the fact that father and son had lost contact with each other during their moves. Fleeing from the Muslims in Baku, Nickolay had not received his father's new address in America. His father could not locate his son because Nickolay had the status of a refugee without permanent address. But the Lord always hears the prayers of His children. And the time came when Nickolay found the true and living God.

His mother, Silva Aramovna, believed first, after she heard the sermons of the Korean-American missionary Yo Han Choi in the Moscow United Methodist Church. She asked her son to come to the service with her every Sunday, but in vain. Nickolay thought it was not serious. From time to time, he went to the Orthodox Church, but could not understand the sermons because the Armenian Orthodox Church uses Old Armenian language, and the Russian Orthodox Church uses Old Slavic. But the children of God kept praying for him. Even if his father or his wife forgot, his sister Aleena prayed consistently.

One day his mother talked Nickolay into accompanying her again to a service. The miracle happened! Nickolay heard the preaching of the Gospel and realized that the things he read and could not understand so long ago were clear now, in all the great wisdom of the Lord. Since then, he never missed a single service. God opened new knowledge in His Word all the time. It was so involving that Nickolay started to read the Bible more and more every day.

Yo Han Choi (after fifty years of pastoral experience) recognized Nickolay's fast spiritual growth and asked him to help during the services. At the beginning, Nickolay was helping with organization, then after he received water Baptism he began to lead the Bible Study. Pastor Choi was already praying that one day Nickolay would accept responsibility as pastor of this church. In May 1995, Nickolay entered the Moscow Theological Seminary. The Word of God was being opened more and more to him. Pastor Choi often asked him to preach during the Sunday services, and on

Saturdays Nickolay preached in a small suburb church in Butovo.

But in the very beginning of his spiritual service, Nickolay went through more trials. His mother died from cancer. Forty days later his niece was tragically killed, and forty days later his cousin died from a heart attack. The deaths of so many close relatives made Nickolay feel much older. His friends and relatives and, of course, Pastor Choi, surrounded him with all care and love, but most help came from the Holy Spirit, who in the Scriptures is named *Comforter*. Nickolay gave himself fully to the service of the church.

After so much suffering, he met his love and future wife Ksenia in the church. She sang in the church choir and participated in the Bible Study. Nickolay and Ksenia got married in their church.

Pastor Choi was using Nickolay more and more for the pastoral service in the Belyaevo church. Soon it was renamed *The Way, the Truth and the Life Russia United Methodist Church.* Pastor Choi, travelling on church business to America, felt confident in leaving Nickolay as his replacement. In 1997, after Bishop Minor appointed Nickolay to be a local pastor, Yo Han Choi ceremonially put on him his own pastor's robe. After graduation from the Seminary, Nickolay was appointed to his home church, *The Way, the Truth and the Life Russia United Methodist Church.*

Yo Han Choi told him as he was getting ready to leave for the United States, "With God's help I preached the Gospel to you, I baptized you, I married you, I made you a pastor. I just need to find your father for you. And believe me, I will do it with God's help!"

Of course, the Lord helped because His children needed help. And the day came when Nickolay was able to call his father on the phone. They both were very happy. Aleena was the happiest of all, because all the miracles in the Dalakyan family began with her prayers. They all were longing for a reunion between father and son, but it was too expensive.

Although for the Lord, who loves His children so much, nothing is impossible! In the summer of 1998, Nickolay went to the United States with a group of other Moscow pastors for a two-week study seminar. The busy time in Kansas City went very fast, and after sixteen years of separation he boarded the plane to go see his father in Seattle, Washington. He was looking forward to telling him all about his first granddaughter Veronica and that they were expecting another one soon. On the plane Nickolay learned that God has a sense of humor. The day of his reunion with his father was celebrated in America as Father's Day!

And that is the story of Nickolay Dalakyan who found his Heavenly Father and his earthly father, his loving wife, happiness to serve for the glory of the Lord, happiness on earth, and the happiness of eternal salvation.

Fyodor Drozhzhin

I will exalt you, O Lord,
For you lifted me out of depths
and did not let my enemies gloat over me.
O Lord, you brought me up from the grave;
you spared me from going down into the pit.
Psalms 30:1,3

If you come to a worship service at the *God's Field Russia United Methodist Church* and listen to its pastor Fyodor, who is a quite respectable old man with a wide beard and a large cross hanging on his chest from a simple chain around his neck, and whose figure shows military stamina, you would never believe that a few years ago he was a homeless and fallen person. He spent nights sleeping in the parks and at the railway stations. He could work hard loading and unloading heavy boxes at the grocery stores for a half-glass of vodka. It was he, Fyodor Dmitrievich Drozhzhin. Former Navy officer, Communist, father of five children, respected by the fellowship. He became a homeless person without a permanent address. Vodka was the only thing to blame.

After demobilization from the Navy, he worked in the administration office of a construction company, later taught in the Technical College, then worked in the Moscow Information Bureau. After perestroika started, he quit the Party. His family, like many others, was having financial difficulties. Fyodor had to work extra to make more money. Often he worked as a laborer, thanking fate for his good health. Sometimes his employers paid him with "natural" products, vodka mostly, and he felt it was okay to drink a little. But as time went by, it did not stop at a little. Glass went after glass, and he became a bitter alcoholic. All the pleading talks of his family and friends did not change him, and as a result, he found himself on the streets—at the very bottom of life. But he kept something special in his soul, and the Lord was able to help him find his way back.

Fyodor was starving, he had an awful stomach ache, and his head was killing him. He could not even remember for sure what kind of liquid he had drunk the day before at the railway station. On that day, he met two of his drunkard friends.

"Do you have anything to eat?" he asked instead of a greeting.

"Do you want a dinner roll with butter and jam on it?" He saw that their hands were empty and thought that they were making fun of him.

"Go away!" he yelled at them.

"We are already going. What about you?"

That winter day his alcoholic "friends" brought him to the worship service of the Korean-American missionary Yo Han Choi. Dinner rolls were given to all in attendance, and Fyodor managed to get two of them! But they were given only after the service. He couldn't stay awake until the service ended, but fell asleep from the warmth and the pastor's nice and kind words.

A new week started with the endless search for a place to spend the night, for work to get some money for food and vodka. But the sermon kept coming back to his atheist mind. He remembered separate phrases and words. The preacher was talking about well-known truths, but for some reason, they sounded different. These words touched him and it turned out he was not asleep all the time, like he thought at first. The sermon was translated by an interpreter and it was hard to concentrate, making him feel tired and sleepy. Also he remembered some other words of the preacher—new, never heard before. Fyodor went back a few more times to that strange place before he understood that those meetings with music, hymns and a sermon, which he had thought to be public lectures, were Methodist worship services. Then he learned that the church was called United Methodist.

Soon, Fyodor was one of the first to the service, sitting quietly in the corner, waiting for the beginning of the sermon. The dinner rolls, so sought by him before, did not mean as much anymore. One time, after the service, he did not leave right away with his "friends" but stayed and talked with other parishioners, people so different from what he had become. The pastor asked what he was doing, puzzled by Fyodor's untidy look. Fyodor did not want to answer but the people around were so kind and honest that he unashamedly admitted that he lived on the streets and was very close to begging from people for the rest of his life. To Fyodor's surprise, pastor Choi did not lose his interest in him and was touched by his story. What happened next, we do not know for sure. Fyodor would not tell us whether the pastor met with his family or he himself went back and repented before them and received their forgiveness. Most importantly, he won over himself and came back to his wife and children.

Fyodor cannot answer the question about when the Lord entered his heart. He cannot name a day which could have been a turning point between yesterday without God and today with Him. It all happened unnoticed. One day, Fyodor came to the realization that he could not go to sleep without a prayer, a talk to God about his day, a thanksgiving for all His gifts.

At the age of fifty-eight he opened the Bible for the first time in his life. And it shook him by the simplicity of its truth, by its answers to all the difficult questions. Yo Han Choi always supported Fyodor in his Bible study, often talking to him and engaging him in the church's work. This included setting up the room for the service and praying or reading the verses from the Bible during the service.

Noticing Fyodor's deep interest in theological studies, pastor Yo Han Choi recommended him for studies at the Moscow United

Methodist Seminary. He was not disappointed in Fyodor. This student became one of the most diligent seminarians in spite of his age. He was one of the most popular people in his class, loved by students and professors. They always looked forward to hearing him preach.

Fyodor was still studying at the seminary when Yo Han Choi began trusting him with the Bible studies and sermons in his church.

On November 10, 1996, pastor Yo Han Choi and student preacher Fyodor Drozhzhin opened a new church in Moscow. It was named *"The God's Field" Russia United Methodist Church.*

Now Fyodor holds two worship services a week: one for his regular parishioners and another one for the blind people, whose fellowship is being sponsored by Fyodor's church.

Oksana Petrova

Ask and it will be given to you;
seek and you will find;
knock and the door will be opened to you.
Matthew 7:7

As did many other technical–scientific professionals, Oksana Petrova became intrigued by the idea of God in the 1980's. It was a time when Russian people received access to literature and knowledge that was closed to them before, and when the ideological censors loosened their grip on mass media. Often, interest in God began with an unexpected meeting which made a person look deep into himself and think critically about his past. A person began asking himself if he had lived his life well, or whether he understood it at all. More and more often the same question kept coming up. Why is it that we are atheists but the rest of the civilized world follows some kind of a religion? They worship Christ, Allah, or Buddha and live with God.

Oksana came to God through her atheist husband, mathematician Yuri. He was fond of works by Hegel, Kant, Bacon, Ilyin, and others. He read the story of Christ's life by Hegel and found out that Christ was God. He realized that human beings could not write such a powerful book as the Bible. It was God's Word. After he discovered it, he shared his revelation with his wife. So, Yuri came to God using his analytical mind and broad knowledge of things. Oksana trusted her husband because he always approached things scientifically.

Oksana finished in mathematics at the university as well, but in philosophical matters she always relied on Yuri. In 1989, friends gave them their first complete Bible. Later, using the philosophers' works and the New Testament Yuri made his wonderful discovery. By the time Yuri and Oksana began to study the Old Testament, Yuri had become a university professor and Oksana was working as a research engineer for the Shipbuilding Institute.

Learning the Bible made them want to attend church. They went to the Russian Orthodox Church but soon found out that it was not the right one for them. After just a few services, they became very disappointed. That church vividly reminded them of the Temple from the Bible where Jesus was so angered by the people. *Then he entered the Temple area and began driving out those who were selling. "It is written," he said to them, "My house will be a house of prayer"* (Luke 19:45,46). So they decided not to go back.

They considered the Baptist church but remembered some bad prejudices they heard about it. Soon after, they met a Finnish missionary who was giving away the New Testament on the streets. He explained to them that Baptists are Christians and the word "Baptist" means "being baptized." But they still did not go to the Baptist church. They were looking for God but could not find the way. It is said in the Gospel of Matthew, though, that *For everyone who asks receives; he who seeks finds; and to him who knocks, the door will be opened* (Matthew 7:8).

The American missionary Bruce Englis came to St. Petersburg and started to, as he liked to say, "plant" Bible Study groups. The Lord helped Oksana to meet that American Methodist missionary. So, Oksana came to the Methodist church where she repented, accepted Christ and was baptized. Soon, she became a leader of the Bible Study group. She realized that she needed more serious training and study if she wanted to understand the Christian faith and her own place in it. She entered the St. Petersburg Christian

University "Logos" and at the same time began learning the English language. She was very successful in her studies.

When another American missionary, Bill Lovelace, came to St. Petersburg, she was able to be his interpreter. Bill also began setting up Bible Study groups and preaching. Oksana was his personal interpreter. Yuri also met Bill. Meeting him changed Oksana and Yuri's idea of American people and helped them to understand Methodism and Christianity in general. Bill had been a mathematician as well and he used to work in a successful company. But during his early thirty's he quit his job and entered seminary in the U.S. Before graduation and starting his new job as a minister, he came to Russia to help with evangelization of Russian people. Bill stayed in St. Petersburg for a few months, and Oksana helped him throughout his whole stay. He could say only two or three words in Russian.

After his graduation, Bill was appointed for missionary service in Russia and came back to St. Petersburg. He hired Oksana as his official translator and interpreter. So, she was a leader in one Bible Study group and helped Bill with the work in many others.

About that time Bishop Reudiger Minor accepted the position of coordinator in the Russian Mission on behalf of the General Board of Global Ministries. He began the process of unification of Bible Study groups and fellowships and churches into the Russia UMC. Only two groups which were planted by Bruce Englis became part of the Russia United Methodist Church: the group led by Oksana and Bill, and Andrey Pupko's church in Pushkin. The others did not join the Russia United Methodist Church.

Oksana, who by then accepted Christ with all her heart, was appointed to be a local leader of *Holy Trinity Russia United Methodist Church*. Bill became pastor of the *First St. Petersburg RUMC*. After graduation from the Theological University, Oksana was appointed a pastor and in 1998, she became an elder in the church. In September of 1993, Holy Trinity Church was registered with the City Department of Justice. It is the official birthday of the church.

Oksana's church became a center of social help and support for many. The members sponsor the Association of the Handicapped called "Boomerang." They visit the homes of the handicapped, bring them groceries and fruits and pray together. Sometimes the donations and help from the American sister churches are not enough, and Oksana gives her own money. Children and grandchildren of the church members attend the Children's Bible Study group. The youth help with music during worship services and participate in English language classes and sports activities together. The most exciting time for the youth is their participation in the church holidays, such as Christmas, Easter, and Pentecost.

Oksana takes part in many national church activities. She is well-known in all Russian churches for setting up the first counseling center for drug and alcohol addicts. The Apostle Paul wrote in his Letter to Ephesians, *Do not get drunk on wine, which leads to debauchery. Instead, be filled with the Spirit* (Ephesians 5:18). During the First Russian Conference of the Russia United Methodist Church her work was recognized by all, and she was asked to be a coordinator for the mission of the Russia United Methodist Church.

Together with the pastor of Pskov UMC, Nelly Mamonova, Oksana was sent to California to participate in an International Conference on the role of the Methodist church in work with alcohol and drug addicted people. During the Conference, Oksana was appointed Director of the Russian Education Program on that matter.

While we were in Los Angeles we were taken to Hollywood and other cities where the centers for work with alcoholics and drug addicts were set up. People are being truly helped there. After I saw these places, I realized how important it was for us to follow their methods. When I began to participate in this work I felt it was God's calling for me to serve those people.

Before my trip I probably would not have noticed, but after my trip to America I saw that one of the new members of my church came to the service drunk. She tried to hide her drunkenness. I asked her to stay after the service and talked to her. Next time, she brought her sister who was a severe alcoholic and had fallen to the very bottom. I prayed for and with them, asked them to come back to the church services and at the same time talked them into having special treatment in the local detoxication clinic. Our church became a partner with that clinic, providing their patients with spiritual help. One of the sisters did not go to the clinic and did not stop drinking. But her sober periods are longer now. Another one agreed to undergo the treatment. She has not drunk any alcohol for a year. Only time will tell if our efforts were successful.

In another example, a new woman came to our church. She seemed to be nice and decent. But one day she couldn't resist taking a drink and came to the next service drunk. So, we learned that she used to be an alcoholic, but had undergone treatment and did very well for a year. We helped her to go back to treatment. Many former alcoholics go through hard times after their treatment is over. But now, they understand that the love of Christ protects them. God is real, He helps those who seeks His help.

The work with alcohol and drug addicted people began in St. Petersburg in 1996. Oksana as National Coordinator helps with the work of the Annual Seminars where people share their experiences. The ministers and doctors from Finland, Sweden, Norway, and the U.S. participate in those seminars. As a result churches in Pskov,

Voronezh and Samara started similar programs. And it happened largely due to Oksana's efforts and hard work.

Oksana also works with the families of addicts. They do not use alcohol or drugs but they are still "co-addicted." They often suffer more than the addicts themselves. They are always in fear whether their husband or brother would come home or not, and whether he would bring home the money or had spent it. Special programs are designed to help families and to teach them how to influence the addicted person. The church in Ekaterinburg has had a lot of experience with such programs.

Oksana and members of her church sponsor the program called "Alcoholics Anonymous." There are about twelve groups in St. Petersburg right now. Alcoholics and drug users spend their free time together and share their stories of failure and success. The Word of God helps them a lot through their trials.

Several times Methodists from sister churches in America invited Oksana to come and witness to them about the story of how Russian people come to Christ. She always accepts the invitation with great joy.

So little do Americans know about Russian spirituality! I felt as if I was a European or American missionary witnessing to people in the African jungles. In my sermons, I have told them about our country, events from my own life, stories about my family and children, as well as about members of my church. They listened so attentively!

Also, they asked me what God meant to me. I told them that God for me is love. I feel it every day in myself and in others. God is my strength. I could not have done anything without God, and my life would not have any meaning. God is the light and warmth in my life, and He shows me the way. God is with me always. I would quote the words of Prophet Isaiah, *Surely God is my salvation; I will trust and not be afraid. The Lord, the Lord, is my strength and my song; he has become my salvation* (Isaiah 12:2).

Olga Ganina

I know that you can do all things;
no plan of yours can be thwarted.
Job 42:2

In 1998, Olga Ganina was invited for the first time to attend the Annual Pastors' Seminar of the Russia United Methodist Church. Only a few weeks earlier she had been formally appointed as pastor of the *Samara Russia United Methodist Church.* For over two years prior to those events, she had been a local leader of the church after Vladislav Spektorov left to attend theological school in America.

It was a total surprise for me. I would have never imagined myself as a spiritual leader. Although I am a very enthusiastic person by nature, I would not have dreamed about becoming a pastor. One time, in the early 1990's, I went to a training seminar for the local leaders of the Methodist churches. After the seminar, Vladislav predicted, "You are going to become a pastor." I did not know why he singled me out, because there were others who attended those seminars who I thought were more qualified. I did not take his words seriously.

Later, during the first pastors' seminar, Olga Ganina met many other persons who were eager to take leading positions in their churches. They did not believe Olga's confession that she asked

Bishop Minor to find somebody else from the *Samara Russia United Methodist Church* to take her place or send another pastor.

The night after I was selected by the Administrative Council to be a local pastor, I could not sleep. I tossed and turned in bed all through the night.

I did not think that I could undertake such a huge responsibility and I certainly could not compare to Vladislav. I was afraid that our church would loose most of its members. I could not sleep. So, I decided to turn to my Bible and just opened it up. The Bible opened on the Book of Joshua. The first verse I had my eyes on read, *Have I not commanded you? Be strong and courageous. Do not be terrified; do not be discouraged, for the Lord your God will be with you wherever you go* (Joshua 1:9). The Lord answered my worries with words from the Scripture! I felt so relieved that I closed the book and fell asleep. My anxiety came back in the morning, but I felt much more confident about my role. I realized that the Lord wanted me to replace Vladislav while he was gone.

The first year passed and Vladislav was still away in seminary. Olga led the prayer meetings, preached, and did administrative work for the church. Nobody left the church as she first feared. On the contrary, many new people joined the congregation. The Children's Bible school was busy with its schedule. The youth group increased in numbers. Two home churches were opened. A new counseling program was set up which was helping people who were addicted to drugs and alcohol. The congregation accepted Olga. Then, the Annual Conference of the Russia United Methodist Church approved her work and appointed her a permanent pastor of the Samara Russia United Methodist Church.

That was when she was invited to participate in the Pastors' Seminar, which she had never attended before. She arrived in Moscow late at night on the day before the opening day of the

Seminar. The first news she heard stunned her. She was supposed to lead the morning service on the very first day! It would be fair to say that she felt a little lost. She did have some experience since she had been a local leader in Samara for over a year. But those were her own people in Samara. It was very different to preach to experienced pastors. Also, she feared that many pastors could be critical toward her since she was a replacement for Vladislav Spektorov, who was experienced and respected by all.

This was her first Seminar, so she did not know about the usual order of the program. She wanted to talk to somebody who participated in the last Seminar. But it was too late at night and everybody was asleep. Olga could not sleep. She was much more anxious and worried than a year ago when she became a local leader in Samara. The Bible did not help her doubts this time. She tried to read it and think of her morning service but nothing came to mind. She fell asleep relying on the Lord for help.

There is a Russian proverb that says, "The morning is wiser than the evening." It was true for Olga. In the morning of the next day, the Lord helped her to pick a topic—"The Love of God." It was simple and well-studied yet appealing to all. The only problem was that the service was going to be very short. It is well-known that it is much easier to preach a long sermon than a short one.

Olga began the service with the Lord's Prayer. Then, she asked everyone to sing a well-known and much-loved hymn "The Love of God is Great." She preached on the passage from the First Letter of Apostle John, *Dear friends, let us love one another, for love comes from God. Everyone who loves has been born of God and knows God. Whoever does not love does not know God, because God is love. Dear friends, since God so loved us, we also ought to love one another* (First John 4:7,8,11).

After the sermon, Tamara Lebedeva led everyone in prayer glorifying Jesus Christ. Then, they sang another favorite hymn, "What a Friend We Have in Jesus." As a benediction, Olga said a short prayer asking for God's blessing on the gathered people. The service was ended with the hymn, "Alleluia."

After the service, everybody went to the cafeteria for breakfast. Olga's anxiety got better only after the Director of the Seminar thanked her for a wonderful worship service. Later, during the Seminar's closing remarks, he reminded everyone about Olga's service, noticing how well she developed her theme and followed it to the end. That first day Olga definitely felt God's grace upon her. She would remember that feeling for a long time.

She came back home to Samara very enthusiastic and full of new ideas and plans. One of the first places she went to was the counseling center for drug and alcohol users in the Pestravsky Region. She wanted to bring the Good News to people, and to help with the remodeling of the facility.

A major part of her motivation, she realized, was that she had looked for God for a long time before she found Him. She knew now that a part of her calling was to present God through Jesus Christ to people before they grew older. Many years had passed, but she remembered her first very tentative meeting with the Lord, when she was a schoolgirl. If only someone had helped her then! She was in the ninth grade, a member of Comsomol (Communist Union of Youth) and a Pioneers' leader for the fourth-graders. One time, she took the kids from her small town to the city of Arzamas to visit some of the famous museums. That city was known for its many Orthodox churches, a few of which stayed opened during the Soviet times. Olga took her Pioneers to the Planetarium, museum and the birthplace of a famous children's writer, Arkady Gaidar. After completing their program, they still had a few hours until the bus trip back home. So, Olga decided to visit the working Mikhailovsky Orthodox Cathedral. She did not try to convert children, but she did sense something special there. She just wanted to take a look in the church at the paintings and icons which were done by famous Russian artists.

One of the children's parents told the school administration about Olga's unplanned initiative. What a mistake that was! Poor girl, she was expelled from Comsomol and almost expelled from school. Her father was called for a serious talk at her school and the local Party office.

Olga's father joined the Communist Party when he was seventeen and believed in its ideas until the day he died. Her mother, although not a Party member, completely shared her father's ungodly ideology. That is why Olga was not baptized, did not know God and later married an atheist.

When Gorbachev's perestroika hit the country, Olga felt lost and empty. She lost her direction in life. During those times, though, she happened upon a copy of the New Testament. The book deeply touched her soul. She took another step toward God when she lost a very close friend who had not been a believer during her life. But before death she repented and accepted Christ. For Olga, these things remained a mystery for a long time. Her path to the Lord was long and difficult. "I think that before death, something important is revealed to a person. But do I have to wait for a serious illness to find God?" she kept thinking.

The Lord helped her through one of her friends, Galina Azina, who invited her to the new Methodist Church in Samara. Galina told Olga that the church was very unusual and the pastor preached wonderful sermons. So Olga came to the worship service of the newly opened Methodist Church in Samara.

Everything was fresh and vital—the concert auditorium of the Music School where the services were held, and the choir that sang beautiful hymns, and the people. They were not just the elderly, like some of the Orthodox churches, but included young people. The words of the sermon talked about our love for others and the meaning of life. They touched Olga's soul so much that she began crying without understanding why. Much later, she realized that her heart opened for the Lord. She asked His forgiveness for the past, for having treated her parents unfairly, and for hurting others. Her soul was cleansed and the tears were not the tears of bitterness anymore.

Next summer, Olga among others was baptized in the Volga River. Bishop Minor of the Russia United Methodist Church and guests from Germany participated in the ceremony. It was very beautiful and solemn. Olga felt for the first time that the Holy Spirit came upon her.

It was such a wonderful feeling, indescribable with human words. My heart felt so joyful and light. I wanted to sing and dance. After the ceremony, we all stayed for a long time and did not want to leave.

From the very first days at the church, Olga began to seriously study the Bible and to participate in many church activities. She helped with the free meals for the poor and the distribution of humanitarian aid. Together with Sister Olga, she helped to establish the Medical Program. Later, she joined the team that worked at the local orphanage. That Children's Home is a very special page in Olga's biography and in the life of the Samara United Methodist Church. The church collects clothing and books for the children and helps with the remodeling and rebuilding of the facility. Leaders of the church study the Bible with the kids and invite them to the services and the church's celebrations. After Vladislav left, Olga began coordinating work at the orphanage as well. Due to her efforts, the Children's Home receives humanitarian aid from sister churches in Ohio and Texas and Stuttgart, Germany. When those churches invited Samara church members to come on a friendship visit, Olga made sure to include teachers from the orphanage in the delegation. Now a few children from Samara are able to spend a year with American and German families and to go to school in those countries.

Olga found her happiness in the service of the Lord. She gives herself fully to Him.

I am so thankful to God that He came into my life and changed it. I am thankful to my first pastor, Vladislav Spektorov, and to my church where I grew and matured in my faith. I am grateful to all my friends and associates who every day help me to follow God's will.

Vladimir Makarov

God opposes the proud but gives grace to the humble.
James 4:6

Everything was well in the life of Vladimir Makarov. He had a great profession as a sculptor, his own studio, lots of orders; and work brought him joy and satisfaction. He was very proud of himself, he could accomplish anything! From gypsum and metal he had created beautiful sculptures that were displayed on town squares or as a part of an interior.

Vladimir has created dozens of sculptures, ensembles and monuments to our soldier heroes which praised the greatness of our people, the winners of the Great Patriotic War. Now they are part of War Memorials and town squares of many towns and cities in the Moscow region. One of his last works, which gives witness to Makarov's fame as a very successful modern sculptor, is the sculpture he was commissioned to do for the tomb of the famous scientist and airplane manufacturer, A.M. Lul'ko. It is in the Novodevichiy Cemetery.

Vladimir remembers,

My very first work, a symbolic sculpture of a worker girl at the gate of the Moscow wallpaper factory, is not impressive. Now it brings smiles or even jokes. It was my very first order and I could not refuse it. I have never made Lenin or any other heads of the State, although those always brought fame. Since

I got established as a sculptor, I have never made anything I did not like.

Pride was always in Vladimir's character—vanity, the desire to create something that would bring him long-lasting fame, not just somebody's monument which would be destroyed as soon as that somebody is gone. Pride was the reason that at forty-five years of age he lost all joy from his work. He decided that there had to be something more to life than just making somebody's images from gypsum. He did not feel any joy at the first public showing of a new monument he had made, or from the success of his exhibits. His soul demanded something else.

In one such moment, he remembered two colleagues—wood carvers —whose names were Ilya and Veniamin. They decorated children's playgrounds together. Ilya and Veniamin were Baptists, very religious people who were so rare to meet those days. They had talked a lot about God and gave Vladimir a New Testament which he never read. Those old talks came alive from the deep corners of his mind and all of a sudden, they happened to be in sync with his mood and thoughts. He decided to turn to God. He did not know yet that *You did not choose me, but I chose you and appointed you to go and bear fruit, fruit that will last. Then the Father will give you whatever you ask in my name* (John 15:16). Vladimir tried to find God in the Orthodox Church. But everything there—icons, paintings, faces of the saints—reminded him of the art he was trying to escape. So, he went to a Catholic Cathedral but the sculptures of the saints again reminded him of his past life. Only after he came to the Protestant church of the Methodist Cho Young Cheul did he feel in harmony with his soul. The sermons, and the possibility of direct talk with God without a mediator brought spiritual satisfaction.

After he had lived most of his life as an atheist, Vladimir Makarov repented and came to God in his mid-forties. He was accepted in the Methodist Church in Moscow, one of the first in all of Russia, which had been opened after seventy years of atheism.

The pastor was the Korean-American missionary and preacher Cho Young Cheul. Vladimir became a member of that church. Later, when the Russian-American-Korean interdenominational Theological Seminary was opened, he became a student.

After graduation, Makarov was appointed to serve as a pastor for the *Thanksgiving Russia United Methodist Church* located in the Moscow suburb of Lytkarino. Again, his life had reached its goal, and everything was going very well. He was happy bringing people God's word. He became exceptionally good at preaching. Many people from other churches came to hear him preach. His church grew. The Government respected them for the humanitarian help the church offered.

Three years passed. Suddenly his vanity and pride returned to haunt him. He left the church where he had found God and was baptized, and went to a different denomination. But after just a few months, Vladimir realized his mistake and repented. He explained what he had done as a trial sent by God.

I had to leave my church, my brothers and sisters, to realize how dear my church had become to me and how close were my ties with the Methodist church.

His story reminded us about the eternal truths of the Bible. After he realized that Satan tempted him, Vladimir repented. He prayed a lot and then, as the Prodigal Son from Jesus' parable, he decided *I will set out and go back to my father and say to him: Father, I have sinned against heaven and against you. I am no longer worthy to be called your son: make me like one of your hired men* (Luke 15:18,19).

To Vladimir's profound relief, the Lord did not let Satan tempt him for much longer. As the loving Father accepted his Prodigal Son, the Administrative Council and later the Annual Conference of the Russia United Methodist Church accepted Makarov back.

Vladimir says

My leaving was needed to cleanse me of my pride, to take all of the worldliness from my heart. I could see my service to the Lord from the outside of the picture, and I realized that my church should be Methodist. It was because of my pride that I thought I was free to do anything I wanted. But no, God's will is for all. All power is from God. I should have listened to Bishop Minor's advice from the very beginning! To understand that, I had to go through the trials. I hope that the dark period is over and I am changed to better serve the Lord.

When the Methodist church accepted Vladimir Makarov back, he opened a new church in Moscow and called it the *Tree of Life Russia United Methodist Church.*

Nelly Mamonova

Humble yourselves before the Lord,
and He shall lift you up.
James 4:10

Nelly Alexandrovna Mamonova is an Elder at Pskov *Russia United Methodist Church.* One time, her son asked her a question: "Mama, can you give me a real example of how the Lord helped you in your life?"

She did not have to think long to give him a positive answer: "Look at your Dad! He denied God. I would give him the Bible, but he would not read it. I asked him to look at the pictures in the Children's Bible, but he did not want to even open it! He told me that I could read all those "fairy tales" myself since I liked them so, but he was an engineer, and he had a different attitude towards life and relied only on himself.

But I am an electro-mechanic myself, and it does not interfere with my being a Christian and believing in God. With time, your father has changed. He accepted the Lord with his goodwill after he saw how much I had changed after coming to God. Before, I was not fair to him, often rude and I never wanted to put myself in another person's shoes. I did not like anything your father did, I nagged him all the time. How could my poor husband stand me?

Only after I came to God, I realized that the Lord loved him as much as He loved me, but I was treating him so badly. I was very selfish. One time, we almost separated. Thank God, He did not let it happen. He gave me wisdom, lessened my pride, and let me see your father from a different perspective. I had changed, so had he. Respect and love returned to our family."

The relationships in the family changed, so did their lives. Nelly's husband realized that it happened according to the will of God. He became very interested in the Bible, and at first rarely and later regularly started to attend the worship services. He repented and accepted the Lord with all his heart. Now, Valery is the first and irreplaceable pastor's assistant. He works as a lead engineer for the Energy Department of the Pskov City Administration and witnesses about God to his colleagues, and tells them about the way he came to the Lord.

Nelly came to accept the Lord as a mature adult. Often people come to the Lord after some kind of tragedy, but Nelly's family was doing very well. Her husband had a great job, so did she. They were relatively well-to-do, and had wonderful children. The eldest daughter was finishing high school and their son was just starting the elementary program. He was growing into a very smart child for their great joy.

By the will of the Lord Nelly happened to meet the very person who later brought her to God. She met Lydia and Irina Istomina, who were among the first Russian Methodists. Raised in a family of Communists, Nelly lived without God most of her life. Lydia, who was a great conversationalist and a persuasive person, was able to change Nelly's heart by her witness. After coming back to her native Pskov, Nelly shared her encounter with friends, and they all wanted to know more about the Protestant religion. Nelly wrote to Lydia and by their request a group of lay people and pastors from Methodist churches in Memphis, Tennessee came to Pskov and held a few evangelization meetings. Pastor James Loftin met with Nelly and her friends and talked to them while preaching and teaching people to pray.

After the Americans went back to the States the interest in John Wesley's teachings did not die. The seeds of faith planted by Pastor Loftin showed some growth. Nelly and her friends kept on with their meetings and tried to read and study the Holy Scripture, to pray and to read spiritual books left by the Americans. They decided to start a church in Pskov.

Nelly took on herself much of the work for the church organization, and everybody accepted her as a leader. Later Dwight Ramsey came to their church and asked Nelly to formally accept a leadership role. So unexpectedly Nelly became a leader of the Pskov congregation. In time Bishop Minor appointed her pastor of the church. She did not know about her talent for preaching and leading other people. More and more people attended the worship services, where they learned about the Good News and the ways they could take part in the life of the community as well. Nelly's special joy was to see many young people, students at local colleges and universities, attend the church.

From the first visits of the Christian friends from the U.S. Nelly's daughter, Katya, became an irreplaceable helper. She spoke very good English and was able to interpret the sermons and speeches of the guests. The Lord brought Nelly's son to church as well. He played the guitar and sang in the Praise Group. Nelly's life became filled with new meaning. She was needed by others and saw it as the greatest happiness. But sometimes, the happy times in life are changed by the not so happy ones.

As a part of an exchange program, a few American students came to the Pedagogical Institute (Teacher's Training Institute) where Katya was studying. Katya met one of them, Michael, at a party, and they began dating. After a few dates, Katya fell in love with the American man. Taking her daughter's feeling very unseriously and thinking of it as harmless flirting without any future, Nelly did not pay much attention to it. But Michael was serious, and after his training was over and he had spent some time back in the U.S. he came to Pskov again. Then, he went back home and the two young people kept writing to each other.

After another year, he visited Pskov again. When Nelly realized how serious it had become, it was too late. She tried to talk to Katya, saying that it would be so unfair to her parents and brother to leave them and go to live in America. But her daughter was firm: "I love Michael."

Nelly could not calm down, everything fell out of her hands. Thank God, the church members were very supportive of her and helped with the church work. Rimma Plyaschenko, Irena Ivanova and others told her to repent in her pride and accept the will of God for her daughter, but Nelly pleaded with the Lord to break the young love.

I was again selfish and strong willed as I was with my husband before I accepted the Lord. But then, I was with the Lord and realized that I kept angering Him. I did not want to listen to anybody and kept saying that I could not give them my blessing. My husband gave in first. I do not know where it would have ended if I hadn't had a vision. The Holy Spirit told me to read Paul's Letter to the Romans, chapter 12, verse 3. I opened my Bible and read, *For by the grace given me I say to every one of you: Do not think of yourself more highly than you ought, but rather think of yourself with sober judgment, in accordance with the measure of faith God has given you.* Only then did I repent. I understood that I could not go against their love and that they both are adults with free will. We all know the commandment given by Moses: *Respect your parents.* But I found another passage in Paul's Letter to Ephesians: *Fathers, do not exasperate your children; instead, bring them up in the training and instruction of the Lord* (Ephesians 6:4). The Lord was talking about a situation similar to ours and I realized that I was too hard on my daughter.

The young couple had a beautiful wedding in Pskov and soon left for America.

When Nelly first learned about The Methodist Church from Lydia Istomina, she was especially impressed by the outreach ministry of the Church. When she became a leader of her own congregation, from the very first days she started a ministry of helping the elderly and the sick. Their sister church in Memphis, Tennessee sent some material help and the members donated some items as well. One of the church's members whose relatives lived in the village of Opochki told the church about the lack of God's Word in that place. So the church decided to start a missionary ministry there. Nelly and others visited the village to hold evangelization meetings. Also, they began sponsoring an orphanage in the Porkhov Region. In the last years, the Pskov church set up a counseling center for alcohol and drug addicts.

Sometimes people would come to the church under the influence of alcohol. Others would go into periods of heavy drinking. Nelly did not push them away but tried talking them out of the harmful habit. Maybe somebody else would have sent them away and simply told them not to come to their church again. But Nelly thought that it was not a Christian way to treat them like that, and she tried to work with them, hoping that the Lord would interfere in their lives.

A very great help in her work was participation in the First St. Petersburg Seminar on the church's ministry to alcohol and drug addicted people. After the seminar, Nelly, together with the pastor of Holy Trinity UMC, Oksana Petrova, went to Los Angeles to be a part of the Conference on the same matters. Nelly spoke at the Conference telling about her work and experience. She learned about the programs used in many American churches such as "Twelve Steps," "Al-Anon," and others. After coming back, she started Pskov's group of "Alcoholics Anonymous" under the church's sponsorship. And the church members who worked with the group began to see the results: some of the alcoholics started on the way to a better, healthier life.

The Lord continuously helps the church with many of their problems. One time, they lost an auditorium for meetings that they had been renting for a while. So, they had to meet at member's homes and in private apartments. But at that time the church numbered over sixty adults and about the same number of children who were divided into three groups according to their age. All those people could not fit into one apartment. The church desperately needed another permanent place. At the same time, the Orthodox Church led an active propaganda campaign against all Protestant churches, so it was very difficult to find a new place. Nelly prayed and a miracle happened.

> I had no idea what to do or where to go. I visited quite a few places but could not find a single one available for lease. One day a church member called. She knew of a suitable room in one of the Youth Community Clubs, the director of which was a young man. I went straight to him, and he readily agreed to lease the room for a very reasonable price. Now, the church has a new place for worship services. And later, we received another of God's gifts. We were able to raise enough money to take out a loan and buy a three room apartment. Our sister church in Memphis and Bishop Minor promised help with the loan payments. In our new apartment we have room for an office and room for the choir rehearsals as well as for the children's and youth group meetings.

Nelly dreams about the church's own building but for the time being thanks God for providing the new place for services and the apartment for other activities and mission work. The Lord gives Nelly many of His witnesses and they help to strengthen her faith and to live in full agreement with herself and her environment. She accepted that her daughter lives so far away, and always waits for her phone calls.

I am thankful to God for making me a spiritual leader, for giving me such a wonderful husband and kids and for everything He does for my congregation and myself.

Nelly repented in her pride and strives never to put herself above others or look at people as if she was superior. She will not pass by the sick, the poor or helpless without giving them her hand of help. She knows from her own experience about the truth of Habakkuk's warning: *See, he is puffed up; his desires are not upright—but the righteous will live by his faith* (Habakkuk 2:4).

Valery Khae

Delight yourself in the Lord
and He will give you the desires of your heart.
Psalms 37:4

Due to God's will or certain circumstances, a leading role in the revival of Russian Protestantism, particularly Methodism, was played by people of Korean heritage. They opened the first Methodist church and the first Methodist seminary in Moscow. Therefore, there were many ethnic Koreans among the first Russian Methodists. They found their calling in service to the Lord. We have already met some of them on the pages of this book, and meeting with others is to follow.

Ten years ago, Valery Ickich Khae was the leading scientist of the Moscow Engineering and Construction Institute. His wife, Galina Tyan, was the head physician of the Pirogovo clinic in Mytischi. They could not even imagine being Christians, much less having responsibility as the leaders of a Christian fellowship. They lived the same as other Soviet families. They celebrated birthdays and tried to fulfill the industrial obligations of the Soviet Five-Year Plan. Valery was working on inventing and testing new building materials; Galina on making her clinic a better place with the best service to patients. In the evenings they would meet in the kitchen and exchange new anecdotes about the people in power whom they had never liked and never believed in. They lived without God and therefore did not have either faith or hope.

God did not leave this loving hardworking family without His attention. The day came when Valery and Galina accepted Christ into their hearts. Today, Valery Khae is an elder in the *Mytischi Russia United Methodist Church*, and Galina is President of the Administrative Council for the Russia United Methodist church.

But even before this the lives of both Valery and Galina, Korean Russians, happened to be happy although their family members had to live through quite a few tragic moments. The roots of both families of Khae and Tyan go back a few hundred years into the history of Russia. Very hardworking, as are many other Korean families, they were well-to-do and certain of a good future. The evil year of 1937 broke the peaceful lives of tens of thousands Korean people who lived in the far east of the USSR. They all were pronounced Japanese spies. Within a one-month period, two hundred thousand Koreans were taken out of their homes, put into cargo trains, and sent to Kazakhstan. They had to leave everything behind.

Thousands of them never made it to their destination in exile. They starved to death or died in the cold train cars, which had been used for transporting cattle. Those who survived arrived into naked steppes and desert. Their habits for hard work let them settle down and start a new life. At first, they lived in dirthouses or even airplane hangars. Later, they built houses. They started collective farms and industry. The Soviet Government did not allow them to leave Kazakhstan until 1953. Only after Stalin's death was their banishment canceled.

Valery's father was very fortunate. In 1937, he was finishing Leningrad University and did not undergo the same repressions as others. They even let him retain his membership in the Communist Party. After graduation, though, he was sent to work in Kazakhstan as well.

After the end of the World War II and the defeat of Japan, Stalin decided to take control over North Korea. Many Russian Korean professionals were sent there for the restoration of industry and "the building of socialism." Among those were Galina's and Valery's parents who were very fluent in the Korean language. In Korea, Soviet specialists were appointed to high positions in the Government as directors and ministers. Valery's father was a professor and Director of the Industrial Institute. He was also head of the Communist Party School. Galina's father started as Vice Minister of Education and later became North Korean Ambassador to Czechoslovakia.

In 1947, both families were sent to Pyongyang. Valery and Galina had just turned six years old. The next year they met for the first time when they entered the first grade of the Russian school for children of Soviet diplomats and military personnel. Ever since, their lives were very close until they became one.

Toward the end of the 1950's, Korea's own professionals finished Soviet industrial schools and Kim Il Sung started to distance North Korea from their "Soviet Brothers." However, instead of being returned to the USSR, Russian Koreans were persecuted again through repressions and exiles. Some of them were sent to work on farms. Others, including Valery's father, were forced into labor in the mines. Galina's father disappeared without a trace. For the families, going back to Russia was out of the question. So, they all had to apply for Korean citizenship. An evil joke was played by fate in their lives. Oppressed in Russia, some survived, studied and worked hard, achieved high positions and then again went through repressions and died in the country of their ancestors. They had given it the best years of their lives.

In spite of their repressed fathers, Galina and Valery had an opportunity to leave Korea for study in Moscow after they finished high school in Korea. Valery entered Bauman Military Technical University. Galina was accepted into the First Medical Institute. During the second year of studies, they got married. Their life was not easy. For a long time, they could not find a place to live together. Finally they found a room in somebody's basement. But their scholarships were only enough to pay the rent and buy a few groceries.

Valery worked extra to meet the needs. Their passionate love for each other kept their spirits up. Both successfully finished schools. Valery went on to graduate school. Galina decided to devote her time to medical practice and raising their son. Valery's mother came back from Korea after the death of her husband. Galina had two sisters still living in Korea.

Years passed, and the couple's life changed for the better. They had their own apartment, bought nice furniture, and lived like many other Russian professionals. Or maybe even better because they had saved their big love for each other.

The daily routine of that happy life was changed forever when an old friend invited Valery to come to a worship service led by a Korean Christian missionary in a newly opened Methodist Church. After that first time, Valery never missed a single service. Many Moscow Koreans along with Russians and Ukrainians came to hear the Word of God. The pastor, Korean-American missionary Cho Young Cheul, opened Bible Study and classes for Korean language study. Valery, who had forgotten much of his native tongue, decided to accept the pastor's invitation to refresh his language skills and to learn about Jesus Christ. As other Soviet people who grew up in Socialist Russia, he did not know anything about God. Many people stayed after class to talk and discuss things with the pastor. Sometimes, they would argue about the meaning of the Bible's verses. Many of them were reading the Holy Bible for the first time.

Cheul was always very patient with us, listening to our childish arguments and explaining his opinions. Most often, at the end we all accepted his point of view. He was always very persuasive. Thanks to Cheul, I came to God. Later, my wife also accepted the Lord. After two years of being in his church and attending classes at the theological seminary, Pastor Cheul suggested that Andrey Kim, Dmitry Lee, and I should start our own churches. Soon, three of the first Russia Methodist Churches were born. The students of missionary Cheul started them all. These churches still exist today, and their pastors became leaders of the Methodist Revival in Russia.

Their churches met for worship services in rented rooms in community clubs, Houses of Culture, libraries and gyms. Later, Valery had an opportunity to rent a building from the Society of Blind and he started a missionary outreach work among that group. The church began helping the blind spiritually and materially. The idea about the church's own building kept coming up. Valery and Galina decided to donate the plot of land they had purchased for building their own house. They had already constructed the basement by then. It was supposed to be a single family house measuring about 26 feet by 29.5 feet. So, it seemed to be a little too small for a church building. They decided to enlarge the basement by about 16 feet in each direction and to take out the one wall that was already built. Pastor Cheul donated a large sum of money for the construction and Bishop Minor added some more. The congregation donated as much as they could. Due to financial and economic crises in Russia, construction was halted on several occasions. But the Lord did not leave them without His help. Later, some people from the USA and Germany became co-sponsors of the project and Russian businessmen helped as well.

Since coming to the Lord, Valery had realized that if one prayed and asked God for something, He would always help. *If you believe, you will receive whatever you ask for in prayer* (Matthew 21:22). There were so many helpless situations during construction of the church that non-believers would have probably stopped and given up. But prayers always helped to find new ways. Valery often felt God's grace whether during church construction or with the problems facing his wife and son.

In February of 1999, the church had its first service in the new building, and on July 4, 1999 the church building was dedicated in the presence of many guests from other Moscow churches and from their sister church in the USA. Before, the church celebrated its birthday in September of 1992, but now they celebrate a new birthday. It is the day when they finished the construction of a beautiful modern building with a sanctuary, rooms for an office, for meetings of the youth and children's groups and choir rehearsals.

The church's choir is one of the best! Valery liked the choir in Cheul's church and promised himself to make sure and have a very good choir in his own, and he does! The choir leader is a Conservatory graduate, Elizaveta Kouranova. The choir has given concerts in all Moscow churches and was invited to many Methodist and Presbyterian churches in Korea, Austria, Germany and the United States.

From the very first day of their service, Valery and Galina gave a lot of their attention to the children of the church. The first members of the children's group are now members of the youth group. Lydia Pronina and Elena Kotelkina finished Moscow Theological Seminary of the Russia United Methodist Church and became pastor's assistants. Elena preaches in Valery's church once a month, and Lydia helps with the services in the second, newly opened Mytischi church. Three members of the first congregation attend evening classes at the Theological Seminary of the Russia United Methodist Church. There are two home churches whose leaders are Lydia Pronina and the pastor's wife, Galina Tyan. There are still many problems and things to do after construction of the building was completed, but the Lord is helping to overcome all of them.

This is the story of the life and faith of Valery Khae, one of the leaders of Russian Methodism, pastor of the Mytischi Russia United Methodist Church. The words of the Apostle Paul in his First letter to Thessalonians could be said about Valery: *Make it your ambition to lead a quiet life, to mind your own business and to work with your hands, just as we told you* (First Thessalonians 4:11).

Alexey Myachin

Blessed is the man
whose sin the Lord does not count against him
and in whose spirit is no deceit.
Psalms 32:2

Alexey's friends always invited him to the Orthodox Church for the christening of their children or for the church ceremonies of marriages or funerals. It was customary to do so in his native village of Kinel'-Cherkassy near Samara. The people there still followed old traditions although the Soviets were trying to purge them from people's minds. Alexey was baptized as a child in the Orthodox Church, and later attended it from time to time. Although his life ways had sometimes crossed with the path of the Lord, he did not take those times seriously. He only began to seek his path to the Lord when he had reached maturity.

All Alexey's visits to church were more like excursions to the beautiful museum of the past, with beautiful exhibits of the icons of Saints he did not know and paintings of Bible stories he never read. For Alexey, the church with its icons, mysterious semi-darkness, trembling light of the candles and the monotonous cries of the priests, "Lord, have mercy! Christ, have mercy!"—all of it seemed to be a living illustration from a history book.

However, as time passed he had to hide even these innocent visits to the church from other people. If known to the Party leaders, one such visit could lead to a serious reprimand or even to an expulsion from the Party. For a Soviet journalist, it would mean a total loss of his career. And it was so distant from the decisions of the last Council meeting of the Central Committee of the Communist Party which Alexey had to cover in the mass media. He did not feel a need to look for a way to God.

Being a journalist, Alexey was fortunate to meet many people of different professions and social status—workers and farmers, Party leaders, other elite of the Soviet Society. He knew people with the most power in the country; he became a very cynical person. He always knew that the Soviet slogan "The Communist Party is the mind, honor, and conscience of our era" was very far from reality. Sometimes during visits with his close friends after a bottle of vodka or at night he would ask himself if what he was doing was responsible and good. But the next morning came, and he went back to his busy life. As they used to say during those times, he was "at the very front of the ideological fight." His titles included editor for the magazine *"Partiynaya Zhizn"* ("The Party Life"), editor for the Central TV station, literature advisor in the procommunist magazine *"Nash Sovremennick"* ("Our Contemporary"), propaganda expert for the mass media main office of the Moscow City Committee, and political educator for the Moscow construction workers.

He did his job thoroughly and consistently as his farmer parents taught him. He grew up in an old and large village in the Samara Region. He always worked hard and was loved by colleagues and supervisors. But he was not happy with himself. He had to lie about something almost every day, make sure that things looked better than they were, keep secrets about others. But journalism was the only profession he knew.

At the age of 62, in 1992, the Lord reminded Alexey—*Believe in the Lord Jesus, and you will be saved* (Acts 16:31)—and gave him a Bible. He had wanted to read it for a long time, but never could. That year, Moscow was filled with missionaries of all kinds of denominations and sects. Each one of them assured people that he was a member of the "true" Christian church. After having read the Holy Scripture, Alexey decided that he needed to learn from missionaries how to live a Christian life.

Alexey remembers,

I did not have much respect for the Orthodox priests. And before I found Methodists I stumbled upon two false Christian communities. The Pastor of one of them told us that our enemies should be three "isms": Judaism, Catholicism and Protestantism. I could not accept that. In another church, a missionary from England said that he came to save Russian Communism from false prophets and assured us that his church was going to lead the parades on the Red Square.

The Apostle Paul talked about such "preachers" in his Letter to Romans, *For such people are not serving our Lord Christ, but their own appetites. By smooth talk and flattery they deceive the minds of naïve people* (Romans 16:18).

Finally, Alexey found The Methodist Church and his path to the Lord through it. He found the truth and led other lost souls with him. He has been serving the Lord for six years now. As many other leaders of the Russia Methodist churches, Alexey finished Moscow Theological Seminary.

While still a seminary student, Alexey started to publish the Russian Methodist newsletter called "Spring." With God's help, it carried the Good News of the Lord's salvation to many people. Through his newsletter, Alexey explains difficult places in the Bible, publishes much material about Methodist beliefs, putting a great emphasis on the fact that Methodists do not consider other denominations their enemies.

Methodists do not fight with either Catholics or Orthodox, either Buddhists or Muslims. Our banner carries the flame which means the spirit of love. We love God and all of His creation. Our path is difficult, but Jesus is our guide and our shepherd. It gives us happiness to overcome temptations of this world with His help. Therefore, there are no people happier than us.

Every Sunday, Alexey holds the services in the church of *"Sunday on Basmannoi."* His home is filled with joy and peace. He has found what he was looking for all of his life. Therefore, Alexey's words—whether on the pages of his newsletter or the words of his sermons for the members of his church—are always devoted to Him alone, our Lord Jesus Christ.

Irena Mitina

*And the prayer offered in faith will make
the sick person well; the Lord will raise him up.*
James 5:15

She is recognized as the "first" Methodist in Voronezh. Irena Mitina happened to be the founder of the church or, to be precise, the first Methodist fellowship, which consisted of seven university professors. It was 1993. Officially, the church was registered a year-and-a-half later after the coming of a degreed pastor, a graduate from the Russian-American-Korean Theological Seminary, Vyacheslav Kim.

Methodism was brought to Voronezh by a group of Americans from the area of Enid, Oklahoma. There were teachers, businessmen, and doctors who wished to learn the Russian language. The lessons were held at the local university. Irena Mitina and a close friend also named Irena were invited as interpreters. Methodist pastors and lay persons, in the providence of God, happened to be a part of the American group. During the time when they were free from their Russian lessons, they held evangelization meetings with the local population and told people about the Methodist Church. Irena helped them, acting as their interpreter.

While visiting all of the missionary meetings and translating sermons, Irena became interested in the faith that was unknown to her. She had been looking for God before, but her search had not been successful.

The Orthodox church left Irena with sad memories. When her mother died and by Orthodox tradition a handful of sanctified Ekaterinburg soil was needed for the funeral, Irena went to the church, where they asked for ten thousand rubles for that soil. It was a third of Irena's salary!

I understand when people have to pay money for candles, wreaths, or other items, which were made by human hands. But they asked such a large price for soil for a grieving person! I felt very strong that that was not the way of Christians!

In another encounter, my ninety-year-old uncle became very sick and asked me to find a priest for his last confession. I went to a nearby church and met a young Father to whom I explained the situation and asked him to visit my dying uncle.

He said, "I cannot come today. Let us do it tomorrow."
I asked, "When tomorrow?"
He said, "Tomorrow at one o'clock. And you will have to provide a car to pick me up."
I told him that I did not have a car and that my uncle lived very close, just five minutes by foot. He demanded that I pay for a taxi, which would take him not only to my uncle's place, but would also wait and take him to the other side of town afterwards! The taxi driver would have asked for half of my salary!
My last question was, "Are you going to charge me for the visit?"
He told me that there was no fixed price but usually people paid him eight to ten thousand rubles. Both of those encounters shocked me. Where was their Christian mercy when they asked money for everything? Such a huge amount of money!

I realize that I was just unfortunate to happen upon those particular priests. Not all priests are so greedy, and one cannot condemn the entire church because of the actions of those two men.

When my mother died I arranged a funeral service for her. I stood there at the church listening to the service, and could not understand a word. I literally needed an Old Slavic interpreter! All of those things alienated me from the Orthodox church, and I decided to look for God elsewhere. At that time, Methodists came to Voronezh with their services. There, I found the Lord. As Apostle Paul wrote, *Faith comes from hearing the message, and the message is heard through the word of Christ* (Romans 10:17).

Later, Irena went to the United States and met other Methodists. Their relationship with the world and with each other touched her. She wanted to follow their example in her Voronezh group, which consisted of her friends and colleagues, professors of the Voronezh University. They studied and discussed the Bible together and argued over difficult matters. The group met in university auditoriums, members' apartments, and even in cafes. Later, most of them repented and accepted Christ.

With the coming of Vyacheslav, and his knowledge in theological matters, Irena's core group grew into the first Methodist Church in Voronezh, the *New Covenant Russia United Methodist Church.* They became more mature spiritually and were ready to undertake outreach ministries, which involved many new members. Pastor Vyacheslav put Irena in charge of the Children's Bible School and the Music group. Irena loved to sing and could play many musical instruments. Work with children always brought her lots of joy. Soon, her skills and love for children made the Bible School the most popular in the city. Many people came to the church through their children. One of them was a future pastor, Igor

Volovodov, who came to the Methodist Church through the daughter of his sister-in-law, Natasha.

When the youth group gave their presentations with spiritual songs and hymns in both Russian and English, Irena always told the audience about the Methodist Church and the ideals of Methodist faith. So their concerts became evangelization meetings which attracted many new members. Some of them came from other parts of the city and had to spend over an hour in transit. So, the Administrative Council of the church decided to meet the needs of their distant members and open another church. Irena was deemed to be the most experienced and theologically educated person, and she was put in charge of the new congregation. It was called the *Resurrection Russia United Methodist Church*, and Bishop Minor appointed Irena as pastor.

The new church was very different from her first Bible Study group, which she led three years prior. This time, it was a real church from the very beginning with regular worship services, prayer meetings, and missionary activities. God helped Irena to rent a wonderful auditorium at the International Club of Spiritual Culture. She was able to create the best Ensemble of Spiritual Music in town. Oleg Pozharsky, a famous composer and poet, undertook the leadership of the group. A professional musician and former Director of the Opera Orchestra, Vsevolod Smirnov played the organ during the Sunday worship services. As before, witnessing about the Methodist church always followed their concerts and choir performances.

Irena started holding separate worship services for the youth in English. All who studied the language and wanted to practice speaking English came to those services. The Bible was read in both English and Russian, and the hymns were sung only in English. The service was held on Saturdays. Once a month Irena let the youth group prepare the Sunday worship service for the entire congregation, which of course is held in Russian. Today the youth group numbers about thirty people. Many of them will be future leaders of the church.

Irena says,
> When I became familiar with American experiences and literature, I realized that one of the most important characteristics of Methodism is its strong emphasis on social justice and charity. I try to follow these traditions in my church.

The results are evident. The *Resurrection Russia United Methodist Church* is respected by the locals for its work in the Regional Hospital and the first City Hospital. Members of the church visit children with leukemia and other blood disorders. They play with them, tell them about the Holy Bible, show Biblical videos, and bring gifts of fruits and sweets.

Together with the City Health Center, the church started a new program called "Healthy Mother." It gives spiritual and medical and often material help to young and future mothers. Also, the church sponsors an AA group. AA usually does not allow anybody outside their group to come to these meetings, but Irena is an exception. The AA members are not ashamed to share their past and present trials with her. Irena talks to them and tries to give as much spiritual support as possible to help them begin a new life. They are so used to Irena's presence now that when she cannot make it, they call her asking what has happened and invite her back to their meetings. The Word of God helps the AA members and gives them additional strength.

"First" in the Russia Methodist Church, Irena started practicing the Service of the Renewal of Baptismal Vows. It is a tradition used in American Methodist Churches for those who were baptized before and want to come back to the Lord, even though it may have been years since they gave evidence of their faith. Three former AA members have been restored and are now active Christians.

A member of the church, sister Galina Kolesnikova, is in charge of another anti-alcohol program called "Al-Anon." It is a group for those who live with addiction, the families of alcoholics.

Together with the other two Voronezh Methodist churches, Resurrection United Methodist Church participates in many other missionary ministries which strengthen the faith and spread the Good News of Christ's resurrection and John Wesley's teachings.

The ways of the Lord are unpredictable. A former Comsomol member and atheist, Irena found her happiness not in the world with its changeable joys but in a life of service to the Lord.

Andrey Pupko

I can do everything
through Christ who gives me strength.
Philippians 4:13

Andrey learned about The Methodist Church from a nice girl's voice on the phone. "Are you Andrey Pupko?" After the affirmation, she continued, "Could you come preach at our church? By the way, we would be really glad to have you as a guest in our home if you wish."

"What church? How did you find me?" Andrey was really surprised by this unexpected request. The girl tried to explain that it was a Protestant church, started recently by an American missionary. She was a leader at the time, but felt that she did not have enough experience in spiritual matters. She had heard from somebody that Andrey knew the Bible very well and could preach, so she decided to invite him.

Andrey grew up in a large Baptist family and attended church from early childhood. As a teen he had been a leader of the youth group, sang in the choir, and played the guitar and piano. Many times he served as Music Director and also witnessed about the Lord during the services. He was loved by all in his Baptist church on Pokrovnaya Gora (Cover Mount) in St. Petersburg. Later, when the new House of the Gospel Church was built on Borovaya Street, the youth group including Andrey was sent to help with the new fellowship.

In everyday life his occupation was "clock master," an expert clock maker. Married and with several children, he earnestly sought to follow the Lord in his life. He and his family thought that happiness would fill their house forever, but one day their calm peace was broken. His wife, although a believer, began quarreling with him for spending too much time in the church. By then, Andrey was a well-known and respected person among St. Petersburg Baptists, and many felt very sorry for him. He did not know how to handle this misunderstanding, and ultimately there was a sad parting.

By the time of the unexpected phone conversation, Andrey had not been in church for several months. At home, he prayed, read spiritual books, tried to talk to God and thought that the Lord had left him. He missed the church family very much. And then, he received the invitation to come to another church. He did not know much about the Methodist beliefs. Is it going to be very different from the Baptist?

"What you are proposing calls for a very serious decision. I need to ask God about it. If I receive a sign from Him, then and only then I will come." This was his answer to the girl.

"What sign?"

"A significant one!"

And the Lord gave it to him. The girl asked him to just open the Bible and read any verse. "Read what the Lord says!"

He thought that that was not a serious way to get guidance, and did not want to do it. But the girl kept insisting and he obliged.

Later, he remembered,

The light in the room was dim, only the night lamp was on. I opened the Bible and the girl on the telephone asked me to read the verse out loud. The years have passed but I still remember that verse. *So get up and go down. Do not hesitate to go with them, for I have sent them* (Acts 10:20).

I just read that chapter a few days ago and remembered that it was a call of the Holy Spirit to the Apostle Paul. After such a sign, I could not refuse and agreed to come. I began preaching in the church which had been started by American missionary Bruce Englis.

Soon another American missionary, Dwight Ramsey, and the Istomina sisters from Ekaterinburg, came to St. Petersburg. They met with Andrey and he became enthusiastic about the Methodist revival in St. Petersburg. They worked together and wrote an Ustav (Regulations) of the church. Then they organized a public meeting which included the members of Andrey's church, the future St. Petersburg First United Methodist Church, and other followers. The meeting participants demanded that the authorities return to them the buildings which belonged to the Methodist church before the 1917 Revolution. The authorities agreed to look into the demands, but could not do anything because some of the buildings had been destroyed, while new apartment complexes replaced the others.

Andrey felt that the Methodist church was right for his beliefs and that the Lord had led him into it. He could not find a good name for his new congregation and asked his mother for help. She suggested "Bethany." There is a small village called Bethany not far from St. Petersburg. And also, Andrey's mother had a picture, "Jesus Christ visiting Martha and Mary in Bethany" above her bed.

In about six months (in August of 1992) the Grand Reopening of the Russia Methodist Mission was gathered in Moscow. Bruce Englis and his assistant and translator, Elena Roukovishnikova were invited. Elena could not come, so they sent Andrey. Irina Istomina spoke and told about her search for historic documents related to the Methodist Church in St. Petersburg at the time of the Bolshevik. She had discovered several of these, and also mentioned Bethany, the Deaconess fellowship which had worked in St. Petersburg in 1917.

Later, Andrey told everybody about his church, and everyone congratulated him on choosing such a great and meaningful name for his church, which symbolized the continuity of history. He had to admit that it was his mother's idea, and neither she nor himself had known about the Deaconess fellowship. It was God's sign. The Conference and Bishop Minor invited Andrey's church to join the Russia United Methodist Church, and he agreed.

Andrey had many other signs from God as well. On one occasion, he was given a pocket Bible by a Finnish friend while he was still attending the Baptist church. Later, his friend regretted the gift. The reason is that tradition dictated the pocket Bible only be given to a Russian pastor through the prayer and revelation of an old priest. When the Finn contacted Andrey to inquire about returning the Bible, you can imagine his surprise and joy when he discovered Andrey was now indeed a pastor. It was a sign from God that Andrey's church was accepted as a traditional and true Russian church.

Another sign that Andrey received was from his future wife. You see, it was her voice on the telephone, challenging her future husband to open his Bible and follow God's will.

On January 7, 1992, on the day when Orthodox Christians celebrate Christmas, the opening service of the Bethany church was held. Ever since, that day is celebrated as the church's birthday.

For over a year Andrey was the leader of his new church, the preacher and the Bible Study leader. Andrey still kept his clock repair shop. It was located in a busy place and gave him a very good income, most of which he spent on the church's needs. On one occasion he paid the rent and bought a new sound system, including microphones, speakers, and amplifiers. But as time passed, Andrey kept noticing that if everything was going well in the church, then his repair shop was failing and vice versa. Combining his leadership of the church and work at the clock shop was getting progressively more difficult. Andrey knew he had to make a decision. It was not easy to turn his back on a business that provided such a good living. But for Andrey, there was no choice, he had to put God first in his life. This decision surprised many people who could not understand giving up such a profitable venture. Andrey stood firm on his decision, trusting in God for his survival. The Holy Scripture says it simply, *Man does not live by bread alone* (Deuteronomy 8:3).

Well, the same day he canceled his license he was paid an unexpected visit by Bishop Minor and the American missionary Bill Lovelace. They came to try to talk Andrey out of his work at the shop and to persuade him to accept the full-time position of pastor. Could it be a coincidence? No, it could not! It was God's plan. Even more, the Bishop offered to refund him for the cost of the sound system. He told Andrey not to worry about anything and concentrate on the spiritual matters, the growth of the new church and reaching out to people. Andrey's first assistant, Lyuba, became his wife and was baptized. Now, she sings in the choir. Sometimes, she replaces Andrey at the pulpit and preaches.

Andrey's experience and skills in reaching people helped him to bring many former atheists to God. Here is an interesting encounter with his neighbor, a former KGB officer. Andrey once asked for help with the room and sound equipment during the worship services. The old Communist agreed, with one condition. He would be glad to help because he had nothing else to do anyway, but he did not want to be converted to Christianity. He said he was raised differently. Andrey accepted the condition. A half-year passed, and the new helper with each service became closer and closer to God. He began to grow spiritually listening and absorbing the Word of God like a sponge. He decided to repent and accept Christ. *For whoever finds me finds life and receives favor from the Lord* (Proverbs 8:35).

In time the Bethany church, through the hard work of their pastor, started new outreach programs as well as missionary work in the Podporozhsky District of the Leningrad Region, which is close to Karelia, and in the villages of Ozera and Kurba. In 1994, Andrey was appointed to be a local pastor, and in 1996, he became superintendent of the North Western District of Russia United Methodist Church. He still serves as pastor of the Bethany church. In 1998, he was ordained an elder. He has much more work now: as a District Superintendent he is a pastor to the pastors of the churches in Vologda, Pskov, Kaliningrad and five St. Petersburg churches. Many leaders of the new congregations came from *Bethany United Methodist Church*. Tamara Lebedeva was recently appointed as a second pastor by the Bishop for her service. Tamara, her sister Galina, and other leaders help Andrey in everything. Their help has allowed him to enter the St. Petersburg Theological Evangelical Academy. He regularly preaches on the Christian radio station "Theos" which is broadcast all over St. Petersburg, Moscow and other Russian cities.

Andrey keeps searching the archives and libraries for materials that witness to the deep roots of the Russian Methodism. Using his own money he photocopied and made into books all of the issues of the first Methodist magazine in Russian, *Khristiansky Pobornik (Christian Advocate)* for 1909-1917. One of those books he gave to Bishop Minor so that the new leaders of the Russian churches were able to learn the history of the beginning and spreading of the Russian Methodism and could use that knowledge in their ministry. Documents which were found and collected by Andrey Pupko helped the Russia United Methodist Church achieve the registration with the Ministry of Justice of the Russian Federation.

Not long ago one more mission was added to Andrey's work. It was a happy one, though. The construction of a new church building has begun in St. Petersburg.

Irena Mukhacheva

It was he who gave some to be Apostles,
some to be prophets, some to be evangelists,
and some to be pastors and teachers.
Ephesians 4:11

It takes a special talent, not just mere knowledge, to teach others. That was how sister Irena was remembered by the members of the Samara United Methodist Church. She was among the very first to help Vladislav Spektorov and Anton Zakharchenko start the church. She was not a pastor although she often preached and witnessed to others.

At the time it was usual to call even much older people by their first names—Sister Anastasia or Brother Vladimir. Despite the fact that she was barely over twenty, as a mark of respect everybody called her by her full name, Irena Borisovna. Her musical talent gave her a special place in the choir.

Children at the Samara church always said that she was the best teacher. Why are we talking about Irena in the past tense? Well, from 1996 she has been sharing her special gifts as a teacher to a different church, the United Methodist Church in Kirov where she was sent by the Bishop of the Russia United Methodist Church. Members of the Samara church still miss her and are very pleased when she comes to visit her native city.

Irena's childhood and youth were typical of a child of the Soviet times. She was a member of Octyabryata (October Children—the Communist organization for elementary school children), the Pioneers, and later she joined the Comsomol. She did very well in school and was a class leader. Later, she was elected a leader of her school's Comsomol organization. While studying in the Institute she was a member of the Comsomol Committee as well. When she finished the Institute and began teaching, she was invited to join the Communist Party.

"I resisted and the Lord helped. Later, I had my children, and the Party leaders did not insist anymore. I told them that I already was doing many extra-curricular activities. I was a member of a Professional Union, a chair of the Society of Young Physicists, and I was working with artistically talented children," Irena remembers.

"Actually, I was very responsible. Anything they asked from me I always did. Only in one thing God gave me strength to refuse: the atheist propaganda. I told my superiors, 'If you think there is no God, why do we need to talk about that at all?'"

All of her life her grandmother remained a deeply religious person, and secretly had Irena baptized when she was a baby. But Irena did not know about that for a long time. Irena grew up as an atheist.

"I came to the Lord through my grandmother's prayers," Irena says. In her visions, grandmother saw Irena with a cross in front of a large crowd following her. She foretold that Irena would be a religious leader. In response to that, Irena only laughed. However, some of her grandmother's visions and tales could not be explained. When Irena was little, houses in the street where they lived were set on fire. The wind was blowing hard and the fire was jumping from one wooden house to another. Irena remembers how the fire was coming close to their house and her parents were taking their belongings out onto the street.

But grandmother would not allow anyone to move her things and stayed in the house. "The Lord won't let our house be burned!" she kept repeating. She did not even look outside and did not know that their neighbors' house was already on fire. "The Lord won't let it happen!" she was saying over and over again.

And He did not! Later, everybody in town talked about the miracle. All the neighborhood houses got burned but Irena's house was a small island in the sea of ashes. The witnesses remembered that the wind did not stop blowing and it was a mystery why their house withstood the fire. The only explanation was grandmother's faith.

The years passed. Irena's grandmother died, and Irena finished the Pedagogical Institute and became a Physics teacher. One year, she was very sick but the doctors could not find what was wrong with her. When the diagnosis of Hepatitis was given, the disease was progressing very fast. Irena's prognosis was very bad and she thought she was dying. She remembers lying on the table in the Operating Room under general anesthesia.

People in white masks surrounded me although I could see only their shadows. My brain was not functioning, and my soul was leaving my body. I was in complete darkness. I saw a white light and heard beautiful music that I had never heard before. The darkness became light and I realized that I was flying. I was in a long dark tunnel moving toward a white light. I could hear voices. I recognized the voice of Professor Rosshchupkin and his assistants, the surgeons performing my surgery. "It is too late. Take her to the morgue."

I was trying so hard to open my eyes and tell them, "No, I am not dead!" But all I could see was the light coming closer. The light spot became bigger and turned into a human face. I was not sure who it was because everything was in a fog. At that moment, Professor leaned over me and asked, "You are alive?!"

Irena woke up in the Recovery room. The doctor was looking at the site of her surgery. "It was a miracle that you survived!" he said. "Your case was almost hopeless."

The nurse who was taking care of Irena replied, "The Lord helped her!"

The doctors and nurse left, and Irena was all by herself. She turned to the Lord for the first time in her life. She did not know any prayers so she just began to talk to God. "Lord! Please, give me more days here to raise my youngest daughter. She does not have a father. Please, help me and ease my pain." The Lord heard her prayers and she quickly recovered. The doctors were amazed but Irena knew that the prayers helped. Much later, she found proof of it in the Book of Proverbs, *For whoever finds me finds life and receives favor from the Lord* (Proverbs 8:35).

When Irena came from the hospital, the first thing she saw was an invitation to come to the House of Youth for a worship service. She was surprised. What could be in common between the Communist House of Youth and a religious service? Next day, she was sitting on the first row of the main auditorium. A man in a nice suit without a cross or icons read verses from the Bible and explained their meaning. The audience was very quiet and consisted mostly of professional-looking adults and young people.

"Was that man who spoke to us from the public education program called 'Knowledge'?" Irena knew all of the lecturers and that man was not one of them. His speech was very precise and easy and everything he said was very clear although he was discussing such difficult matters. Irena herself had puzzled over them many times. Only towards the end of the meeting she realized that she just heard her first sermon given by a missionary. She still remembers that sermon, although she had a chance to listen to many missionaries and theologians over the years while in the seminary and during conferences.

At the end of the service, the audience was invited to pray. The prayer was very different from her grandmother's prayers where each third sentence was "Lord, have mercy!" After the prayer, they all shook hands and hugged and exchanged greetings and wishes of good health. It all was very unusual and interesting.

Next Sunday, Irena learned that the church was called Pentecostal and "the lecturer" was pastor Vasily Lyashevky. She began attending the church on a regular basis. Soon, the pastor noticed her attendance and invited her to come to the Bible Study during the week.

Later, she began speaking to elementary school children at the school where she taught Physics. She called her lessons "The Lessons of Morality." Seven- to ten-year old children were eager to hear the Bible stories and to learn about God.

The Bible Schools were appearing those days like grass after a rain. During seventy years of the Communist regime people became hungry for true ideals, spirituality and the Word of God. Irena met the Methodist group led by Vladislav Spektorov and Anton Zakharchenko. Later, she joined them. Vladislav was a wonderful teacher, who knew and explained the most difficult places in the Bible as well as the teachings of John Wesley, the founder of the Methodism.

After Vladislav got to know Irena better, he asked her to teach the Bible School at the Samara Children's Home, which was sponsored by the church. Irena always loved to be with children and fully gave herself to her work. After joining the Methodist church, she kept visiting the Orthodox church, the Pentecostals, and other Protestant churches.

"In the Orthodox Church," Irena remembered, "old women kept correcting me, 'You did not stand right.' 'You did not put your candle correctly.' 'You put a wrong scarf on your head,' and so on." And it was beyond me to understand what the priests were saying.

Vladislav was never against my visits to different churches. "Let her visit others," he used to say to the church members who did not understand me. "She is gathering knowledge."

Irena's faith was growing with each passing day. Doctors found her liver to be completely normal and even doubted the need for the surgery which had already been performed. However, Irena knew that together with the Lord she had won over disease and death. The Lord healed her.

After listening to Vladislav's sermons and getting to know the teaching of John Wesley, Irena realized that she liked the Methodist Church the most. She was very thankful to the Pentecostal church, because they brought her to God. But the Methodist teachings attracted her by their simplicity. She became an active member of the *Samara Russian United Methodist Church.* She read, prayed and witnessed a lot. Vladislav recognized her hunger for knowledge and sent her to the Tallinn Theological Seminary.

After finishing the seminary, Irena came back to Samara. In Kirov, a Methodist fellowship had been started by a group of lay people and clergy from the Dothan (Alabama) and Marianna (Florida) Districts of the United Methodist Church in the United States. But no local leadership had developed from the large group of Russians who had been meeting with the Americans. So in 1996, the Samara RUMC sent Irena to work with that fellowship.

She decided to begin with the youth and students of local colleges and universities. The first meetings were held in her apartment with ten to twelve people present. She was preparing the new leaders of the church from her first students, and she succeeded! In a few months so many people wanted to learn the Bible that they had to form several groups.

Young people asked how to live with God, how to hear the Holy Spirit and how to pray. Irena did her homework very seriously. She now thinks that if she were not in Kirov, but in her native Samara, she might not know all the answers to the difficult questions she was asked.

When the church in Kirov was opened, another couple from Opelika, Alabama, John and Cynthia Knowles, came to help her. John began giving English lessons to everyone in the church who wanted to study with him and to hold worship services. Irena contacted the president of a local university who agreed to allow the church to use the university auditoriums for services with foreign guests or when Bishop Minor comes to visit.

Irena's apartment became a second home for many students. Many of them call Irena their Teacher of Life. Irena herself refuses such a great title and quotes the Bible, *But you are not to be called 'Teacher,' for you have only one Master and you are all brothers* (Matthew 23:8). Now, the church has its own place where they hold Sunday services.

The church's authority truly increased after the miracle of Irena's healing. She was renting an apartment from the Seleznevs family, who were members of her church. They asked Irena to visit their terminally ill mother, Vera Nikitichna. Although she was a zealous atheist, her children hoped that she would come to God before she died.

Irena realized that her visit was going to be very difficult. Vera Nikitichna had been a Communist all of her life and viewed religion as "a poison for people." Even though she was terminally ill and could not walk or live without others' care, she refused God and any religion. Irena knew that it was going to be a hard task to change the old woman's heart. However, as a pastor, she had to give it a try. She knew that if she failed, she would fall in the eyes of her congregation. So she prayed a lot and asked the Lord to go with her.

Vera Nikitichna greeted Irena with a declaration of her own poetry, which sang praises to Lenin and the Communist ideals. Irena could barely interrupt, "It is all written in the Christian Commandments!" But the old Communist knew about that. She was not going to let it go easily. She kept interrupting Irena with cunning questions. However, Irena always gave wonderful answers. During the next few visits, the Lord was speaking through Irena. She quoted the Bible to the last letter not even opening the book, which made Vera Nikitichna convinced in the truth of the Word of the Lord. The old woman asked how to confess, how to pray and how to accept Christ. Irena Borisovna herself was once again assured in the right choice of her path. *I can do everything through Christ who gives me strength* (Philippians 4:13).

After those visits, Irena had to go back to Samara for a few months. The church kept their meetings under the guidance of the local leaders. When Irena came back to Kirov, a greeting party from her church members was assembled in her apartment. The first person Irena saw was Vera Nikitichna standing there. Just a few months earlier, she could not even get up from her bed and was expected to die very soon. Now, she came to greet Irena from the other side of town! Was it not a miracle?

"Vera Nikitichna, is it you?" was all stunned Irena could say. She could not believe her eyes. The old woman's daughter who studied the Bible in Irena's church reminded them of the words from Apostle Paul's Letter to Romans, *Everyone who calls on the name of the Lord will be saved* (Romans 10:13).

When Irena Borisovna came to the first worship service after her long leave, she saw many unfamiliar faces. They were new members of the *Kirov United Methodist Church.*

Yuri Sokolov

Turn to me and be saved.
Isaiah 45:22

Yuri grew up in a family of alcoholics. It seemed like the Lord had turned away from his family. When he was twelve years old he began to use drugs and later alcohol. At eighteen, he got married to a girl whose family—father, mother, and siblings—could not live a day without alcohol. His wife was the only one whom the Lord saved from this harmful addiction. She could not understand what kind of joy people found in drugs and alcohol. If she had known that Yuri used drugs and had long drinking periods, she would have never married him. She found out about it when they were expecting their first child.

The next six years were very hard for her. Although they had two daughters, and somehow Yuri had acquired a good occupation as a cook, a machinery operator, and a driver, alcohol was the constant reason for all problems in their relationship. But the day came when the Lord made Yuri stop and think about his wife and children, and to look back at his life.

Two events happened prior to that day. The first was meeting a South Korean missionary; the second was a desperate prayer by Yuri's atheist wife. She fell on her knees and prayed, "God! If you do exist, bless my husband and save him from vodka and drugs. I left my parents' house and cannot bear to see it in my own family!"

Much later, Yuri would realize that the simple prayer of his wife changed so much in his life. From that day, he stopped using drugs, and later, was able to win over his addiction to alcohol. The Word of God did not reach him right away, but the Holy Spirit continued the work of saving the young man from Satan's web. Although Yuri tried hard to fight his addiction, he never was successful. He understood that there was another life which was passing him by. But Satan's powers were too strong over him.

Yuri could not tolerate it when somebody tried to teach him and criticize his way of life. A missionary from the Pentecostal church found amazing words to tell Yuri about the meaning of life, about the love of God. That loving missionary did not try to tell him that alcohol was bad for his health, or to make him stop using drugs. Those loving words touched Yuri's heart.

After a few meetings with the missionary, Yuri became an attendant of the Theological Seminary of the Assembly of God Church. Bible lessons and sermons of the missionaries took Yuri into a new unknown—a life where people loved each other, honored the elderly, and respected others. Outside of the seminary walls he saw the same old life he was trying to escape. Evil, hatred, hopelessness and alcoholism were still waiting for him at every turn. Old friends called him to join them, and Satan continued to tempt. Sometimes Yuri could not fight those temptations and turned to alcohol. But then he would return to the seminary and to God and give himself a promise not to go back to the past anymore. He clearly understood that there was a different life which he could have if he accepted Christ and lived by His word. He repented and the Lord forgave him.

At the seminary Yuri met another Korean missionary, a Methodist named Sing Hung Moon, who became interested in Yuri and began helping him with preparation for the ministry. At first, Yuri did not understand why his pastor thought and hoped that the former alcoholic would be able to become a pastor himself. But S.H. Moon was able to see the future missionary in an alcoholic, who had just chosen the right path in his life.

I loved talking with Moon. His words touched me. Just like him, I wanted to go to people and open up the truth for them, "Poor people! You live in darkness and do not know the Lord, who loves you! You do not know about the life eternal. Think about your future." The book of John Wesley's sermons especially touched me. I was eager to continue his work. With each passing day, I could feel the influence of the Holy Spirit in my life.

At the age of twenty-four, Yuri Sokolov repented and came to the Lord after many wasted years. Yuri did not have any cravings for alcohol or drugs any more. When he met drunken people, he felt sorry for them. What did they know about real life, life with the Lord? When Moon became assured that Yuri was firm in his faith and would not go back to the past, he began trusting Yuri not only with the preparation for services but with public praying and preaching as well. In 1997, pastor Moon started a new church, and Yuri became a leader of Moon's first congregation. For the first two years, he was serving as a local leader, and later was appointed as pastor. There were over twenty adults and about twenty children in his congregation. Yuri opened a Bible School for adults and together with his wife he holds Bible classes for children. His wife helps him a lot. She also accepted Christ in her heart. Now, the spirit of peace and harmony reigns in their family.

They are raising two daughters and a son whom they adopted from the orphanage. The child was born with Cerebral Palsy and abandoned by his parents. Yuri's family takes care of the boy and prays for his healing. The church, which Yuri called "Light," sponsors the orphanage.

We spend on the orphans all money we receive from sponsors or donations. We buy clothes for them, shoes, textbooks, fruits, and vegetables. We bring them religious materials as well. The Government does not pay the orphanage even a third of the promised budget. If not for our help, the children would have to beg on the streets to survive. I show them religious videos and tell them about Jesus Christ. We read the Children's Bible together. I have such a joy in my heart when I see how eager kids are for the Word of God and accept Christ in their young hearts! Children are the foundation of the future of Russia. I realize that and give them more attention than adults. People of the city gave me a nickname — "Children's Pastor."

Members of Yuri's church began missionary work in the villages around Khabarovsk. They have already opened a new church in the village of Nickolaevka. The village administration let them use one of the buildings. Now, they hold Bible lessons and prayer meetings there.

Korean missionaries gave "Light Church" a three-room apartment in Khabarovsk for the church office and meetings of the youth and children's groups. By the decision of the Administrative Council that apartment was exchanged for a private house, which was remodeled by the congregation. Now, they have a place for worship services and meetings.

There are more than ten independent Methodist churches started by missionaries from South Korea, Australia and New Zealand. They are not a part of the General Board of Global Ministries of the United Methodist Church. Until May of 1998 Yuri's church was not a part of that group, either. After having attended the Annual Conference of the Russia United Methodist Church in Moscow and talking to other Russian Methodists and Bishop Minor, Yuri put in a request that his church be accepted as a part of the Annual Conference.

I am so glad that our church is under the jurisdiction of the Russia United Methodist Church. Now, I have an opportunity to exchange experiences with leaders of other

Methodist churches. We participate in seminars and live in one spirit with other Russian and world Methodist brothers and sisters.

When Yuri was a child, society did not do anything to save him from the harmful influence of his family. When he grew up, society turned its back on him. But the Lord sent him a wife with the same sad story, who realized, that *Wine is a mocker and beer a brawler, whoever is led astray by them is not wise* (Proverbs 20:1). Since Yuri repented, accepted Christ, and became a pastor for others, he often talks about alcoholism in his sermons. The Apostle Paul wrote in his Letter to the Ephesians long ago, *Do not get drunk on wine, which leads to debauchery. Instead, be filled with the Spirit* (Ephesians 5:18).

Yuri is doing his best to help and save his as well as his wife's parents, but Satan has a strong hold on them. Yuri is very hopeful that with God's help he will be able to bring his parents to God. For now, he gives himself fully to children, his own and the others, and brings the Good News to other people, who have not found God yet but desperately need His salvation.

Vera Agapova

Though you have made me see troubles, many and bitter,
You will restore my life again . . .
You will increase my honor and comfort me once again.
Psalms 71:20,21

American tourists often came to the old Russian city of Vologda, but this time it was a Methodist group from San Antonio, Texas, with the Peace Foundation. Vera's husband Sergei worked for that organization and as interpreter he escorted the American group in their tour of the city. Sergei was fond of philosophy and the history of different religions, so he really enjoyed meeting new friends. During the evangelization meetings, Scott Somers captured him by his knowledge and charisma, and Sergei invited him to stay with his family. That was when Vera met him for the first time.

Vera learned about the Methodist faith in her own home for the first time through that American pastor and missionary. He stayed with Sergei and Vera for a few days. She was not interested in either Americans or religion; she was an atheist. But when the American pastor came to their home and she had a chance to talk to him, she became very interested in the matters of faith.

Scott told her many interesting things about John Wesley and about God. He spoke to Vera differently, like no one had ever spoken to her about God before. Sergei was charmed by their guest and led long discussions about the Bible which he had read years before, but as he found out did not understand correctly. Scott explained it to him very eloquently. Vera was listening to those talks as well.

The Americans left, but their evangelization efforts had touched the hearts of the people. Close friends of Sergei and Vera's began to meet and read the Holy Scripture together, discuss the topics which Scott helped them to list before he left, and pray. With those small meetings, the church in Vologda began to be established and naturally, Sergei became its leader.

As the group grew they were able to officially register and Bishop Minor appointed Sergei to be a temporary pastor at first, and later a full-time pastor.

Sergei enthusiastically started to spread the Good News and brought many new people to God including young people. He preached not only in the church but also at the schools and among college students as well. Vera did not attend every service at first, but later she became used to it and could not imagine a Sunday without God and her husband's sermon. Sergei tried to get her involved in the work of the church, in the service and room preparation as well as working with children

Vera remembers when she read the Bible for the first time,

Long before the Americans came to stay with us, Sergei read the Bible. I remember he was reading the same big book for a few weeks, so I asked him about it. He showed me the cover, *Holy Bible*, and said, "You should read it and then you would understand why a person can read this book all of his life and never finish reading it." I tried it and although everything seemed to be simple, it needed lots of explanation. I would open up a page, pick a verse and ask my husband to explain. Sergei always did his best, but sometimes he did not know the answer to my question and began to search for it. I could have never imagined during those times that one day I would become a pastor and would lead other people to Christ. But it did happen.

In 1997, Sergei was killed in an automobile accident, and his church was left without a pastor. To make things worse the City officials refused to allow the Methodists access to the building they were renting for their services. Vera had to replace her husband and lead the church. They began meeting in her apartment. Thank God, it was large and could hold about twenty people. The youth had to meet separately at a different time.

If not for the Lord, who has first place in her heart, Vera does not know if she could have had the strength to survive. She read the Bible which helped her a lot, especially this verse from Paul's First Letter to Thessalonians, *Brothers, we do not want to be ignorant about those who fall asleep, or to grieve like the rest of men, who have no hope. We believe that Jesus died and rose again and so we believe that God will bring with Jesus those who have fallen asleep in him* (1 Thessalonians. 4:13,14). She remembered the other tragic days when her Dad died and Sergei tried to comfort her and her mother, telling them, "Why are you crying, feeling sorry for him? It is much easier for the ones who are gone, especially if they were righteous people. It hurts more for those who stay."

Her close friends, sisters and brothers in faith, helped her to live through Sergei's death. Bishop Minor and GBGM Coordinator Jarrell Tyson came from Moscow. The Northwestern district superintendent, Andrey Pupko, came from St. Petersburg. They held a funeral service for Sergei according to the traditions of the Methodist church. In a few days the missionaries from America who helped to start the church also arrived in Vologda. They tried to comfort her the best they could and were able to persuade her to continue her husband's work.

They took her to Moscow to talk to the Bishop. After a long talk with Bishop Minor, Vera agreed to replace her husband in his ministry. The Bishop blessed her for the service and in two years Vera was appointed a local pastor of the *Vologda Russia United Methodist Church* at the Annual Conference. As Vera used to help her husband, now she found a great help in her son Constantine. He became a youth group leader.

The church sponsors the orphanage school and helps them with repairs and gives spiritual and material support. A wonderful quartet was started by the young church members. They play not only in the church but also in schools and other places. Young musicians bring teachings of the scriptures and of John Wesley, together with musical pieces and hymns, to their audience.

The ministry to God helped Vera Agapova live through her personal tragedy and to begin a new life, together with her son. She devotes her continuing life in ministry wholly to Him, realizing in her heart the truth of these words, *give thanks in all circumstances, for this is God's will for you in Jesus Christ* (1 Thessalonians 5:18).

Vyacheslav Kim

But seek first his Kingdom and his righteousness,
and all these things will be given to you as well.
Matthew 6:33

If you get to hear Vyacheslav's wise sermons about the meaning of life and about prayer and how to pray, you would be surprised to know that only ten years ago he did not know anything about God and was a convinced atheist.

"Yes, it is true," Vyacheslav says, "I came to church before I believed. I learned about the classes of the Korean language and came to them. Later, I did not notice exactly when I came to the Lord."

Vyacheslav's life always had been great and happy. He finished the Institute with a constructor's degree and worked in Moscow. Later, he received a Master's Diploma and stayed at the Institute in a teaching capacity. While working on his Master's he met his future wife, Marina. He never had a reason to complain about life. People often turn to God when something bad happens. In the Kim family, everything was going well.

When perestroika happened and the iron curtain was torn down, people remembered their national conscience and family traditions and became interested in their family tree and the history of their nations. It was the same for Vyacheslav. When he heard about the newly opened classes of Korean language study he decided to give it a try.

Cho Young Cheul, an American-Korean and a Methodist missionary, started those classes. As Vyacheslav realized later, Cheul's main objective was spreading the Christian faith in Russia. When Cheul asked Vyacheslav if he was a Christian, Vyacheslav gave him an unambiguous response. He said that he did not want to learn anything about Christianity and that he was interested only in the language. Cheul replied that it was fine. The lessons consisted of three parts, including Grammar, history of the Korean culture, and Bible Study. Students could attend any or all three of them.

At first, Vyacheslav attended only the language part and left when that was over. Then he became interested in the culture of his ancestors. He enjoyed meeting people of the Korean nationality. Many of them had lived lives similar to Vyacheslav's. All of the Russian Koreans who met at Cheul's church belonged to the families of those who were sent from the Far East to Middle Asia by Stalin's Government. Vyacheslav never knew that there were so many Koreans in Moscow. It seemed like all Korean descendants in Moscow attended Cheul's classes.

Soon the lessons became a place where students could meet many new Korean friends. Shortly after that, two lessons were not enough time for having fellowship and many began attending the worship services as well. The teachers of the language class took their responsibility and their mission very seriously, although all of them were volunteers. When someone would explain something in their action or attitude by their faith in Christ, Vyacheslav viewed this as pure propaganda. However, he felt very thankful to Pastor Cheul for everything he had done to restore Korean national identity in Soviet Koreans. They had lost it during the seventy years of the Soviet regime.

Vyacheslav was truly excited with his new acquaintances. He did not take seriously anything he heard during pastor Cheul's sermons for quite awhile. However, from time to time he started to think about the simple truths he remembered from the services. One of the last turning points in his life was an unexpected reading of work by the Orthodox priest Father Alexander Men.

> One day, I came home to find my wife all in tears. I asked her what had happened.
> "They killed him! They killed him!" she kept repeating through tears.
> I was scared. "Who is killed? Someone from your family? From mine?"

It turned out that an Orthodox priest, Father Alexander Men, a popular figure among many educated people in Moscow, had been murdered. At first, I did not even realize who she was talking about or why she was so upset.

I became angry, "What was he to you? A relative? It is not such a loss to have one priest killed! You would have been less upset if I died!" I was very jealous and angry because I had never seen my wife so upset before. I knew that she listened to Alexander Men's radio program and was one of his fans. I think she became a Christian after listening to Men and reading his books and sermons.

The argument with his wife ended with Vyacheslav deciding to read Men's books himself. He wanted to prove that they were a waste of time. But when he began reading, each page opened new horizons for him. It opened what was previously unknown to him, the realm of God. He was stunned! He had always thought that God and religion were for fools and uneducated people. But it all was much more serious. Vyacheslav came to accept Men's ideas and share his points of view.

Alexander Men's books helped to change not only his mind, but his soul. He understood and shared Father Men's words, "Christianity is not a new ethics, but a new life, which brings a person into initial touch with God. It is a new union, a New Covenant." Father Men helped Vyacheslav to realize the deep meaning of the revelation of Jesus Christ from the Gospel of John, *A new command I give you: Love one another. As I have loved you, so you must love one another. By this all men will know that you are my disciples, if you love one another* (John 3:34,35).

Vyacheslav remembered,
> Those words penetrated the deepest corners of my heart. I was shedding tears of repentance. My soul was changed and I turned to God with my confession of sins. Ever since then I have listened carefully to Cheul's sermons and opened for myself new depths of the Lord's teaching.

On November 26, 1991, Vyacheslav was baptized in the Methodist Church. He accepted Christ as his Savior and decided to serve the Lord. The next year he entered the Interdenominational Theological Seminary. While a student he served as a local pastor in Mytischi United Methodist Church where he first experienced being a real pastor. He will always remember the warmth and love he was given by that fellowship and its leaders, Valery Khae and Galina Tyan. Vyacheslav's personality as a pastor was greatly influenced by three people: pastor Cheul, missionary Kim Song Lee, and Bishop Minor. The Bishop helped Vyacheslav realize that the main objective of the Methodist Church in Russia was to become a Movement of Revival and an instrument of the coming Kingdom of God in this world.

After finishing seminary, Vyacheslav was appointed as pastor to Voronezh, his wife's home city. So the whole family met that appointment with great joy.

On November 27, 1994, Vyacheslav opened Voronezh's first Methodist church, called "New Covenant." It was opened on the foundation of the group led by Irena Mitina. In a year, Vyacheslav was ordained a deacon. Working in the church, he realized the lack of his knowledge of human psychology. So, he entered Voronezh University's department of psychology.

His newly acquired knowledge proved to be very helpful. It was perhaps most helpful while working in the Therapy and Psychology Center for teenage drug-addicts. Now the work against drug and alcohol addiction is an important part of the church's outreach ministry. With the church's initiative and the Bishop's blessing, the International Humanitarian Center, "Grace", began its work in Voronezh. The mission of the Center is spiritual and educational work in the matters of health, culture, education, arts, science, and forming of the national conscience on the basis of Christian ideas and national traditions.

The numbers of church members attracted by Vyacheslav's sermons consistently increases. So now the New Covenant church had two daughter churches, *Resurrection RUMC* and *Apostles Peter and Paul's RUMC*. Vyacheslav's students, Irena Mitina and Igor Volovodov, became their local pastors. Vyacheslav always gives them a lot of help and support. All three churches work in close cooperation and try to cover as much of the city as possible with their outreach ministries.

In 1998 Vyacheslav was ordained an Elder and the next year he was asked to serve as Superintendent of the new Central District of the RUMC.

Sergei and Irena Kovriginy

Two are better than one,
because they have a good return for their work.
Ecclesiastes 4:9

Sergei is a pastor in the newest St. Petersburg Methodist church—*Martha and Mary RUMC.* His wife, Irena, is pastor's assistant. They both are theologically educated. If needed, Irena can prepare the service and preach. Their small but growing fellowship consists of over twenty adults and a few children who attend Irena's Bible Classes. There are also a few youth who have become a part of this church family. However, services are mostly attended by older people. Sergei and Irena are very enthusiastic. They plan a lot of different activities to attract younger people.

Since Sergei speaks both English and German, one of these activities will be opening a foreign language class. The youth will study German and English through Bible texts and hymns. The pastor is already starting to put this plan into action. Right now, they spread the Good News by distributing fliers on the streets, inviting people to their services as well as concerts of spiritual music and poetry. Young evangelists sing and play musical instruments, Sergei writes poetry. Also, they invite Christian musicians from other churches. They have established a good relationship with the Musical Group led by Oleg Pozharsky from the Voronezh church.

They hope to start a marriage counseling program called "Nove-Shalom," which means "good peace in the family." Two Americans, Michael and Marilyn Philips, created the program. It is designed to help create a healthy family atmosphere and solve any existing problems in the marriage. Sergei and Irena took a training course and are able to teach and counsel others.

Martha and Mary RUMC takes an active part in different programs in cooperation with other St. Petersburg churches. These include broadcasting over the Christian radio station "Theos" and hosting Children's Christian Summer camps.

Both Sergei and Irena were raised in atheistic families. Irena says,

I was raised in the spirit of Communism, with faith in their leaders. Only later I realized that the leaders of the Party were not sincere people. Most of their ideas were taken from the Bible and changed to serve their own selfish purposes. I thought that with the fall of Communism I would be rid of falseness and insincerity.

But in the early 1990's, Voronezh, where the Kovrigins are from, was filled with all kinds of fortune-tellers, shamans, and occultists. They all "preached" spiritual and supernatural things, and the Kovrigins thought that they were close to God. Thank God, He saved them from those false prophets. Sergei and Irena came to God through the Baptist church. Later they met some charismatics and loved their upbeat lively music. So, they began going to their services.

Irena remembers,

My Grandmother planted a little seed of faith. My feelings about God were always ambivalent. I knew that He existed but at the same time, I was not a believer. I was raised as an atheist. While in school, I visited the Russian Orthodox Church a few times, but it did not bring me any closer to God. Nobody was interested in me, no one tried to talk to me and ask why I was there and what I was seeking. So, I stopped going.

Later, I met Baptists, and they were different! They asked where I was from and why I was looking for God and wanted to know more about me. They brought me to the Lord.

Sergei was fond of reading about the supernatural. He had a large collection of newspaper and magazine clippings about poltergeist, UFO's and other similar things. That interest in the unknown was something in common between Sergei and Irena when they first met. They fell in love and started their journey toward the Lord as a couple. Sergei was the first one to acknowledge God in his life. When he came to Voronezh, he found a room for rent with a Baptist family. The father, a deeply devoted Christian, heard about Sergei's strange interests and began witnessing to him from the Word of God and talking to him about the Christian faith. He talked Sergei into reading the Bible. Page after page, Sergei began reading it every day. He also read all other Christian literature his teacher could find for him.

The day before Sergei promised to go to the Baptist church, he happened to find a small book at the bookstand. It was called *Crossover, The Last Illness, Death and After-death* by Pyetr Kalinovsky. For some strange reason, Sergei liked the book and bought it. He kept reading it until he reached the end. The author was a doctor and a very devoted believer who proved by examples that death was not the end, and that the soul does not die but keeps on living in a different world. He talked about many people with near-death experiences, with quotes from famous people. They told about the feelings when their body and soul seemed to separate from one another. After Sergei finished the book, his last doubts about going to the church were dismissed. He went to the Baptist church, repented and accepted the Lord.

He remembers,
I felt unexplainable peace. Calmness and confidence replaced all my fears. After I met Irena, I brought her to the

church and persuaded her to get baptized. The Bible was very hard to understand for her as well as for myself. But instead of the Old Testament books or the Gospels she began reading the Bible with the Book of Revelation, and all of its prophecies scared her. It took our pastor and me a long time to help her with the reading of the Holy Scripture.

After graduation from nursing school, Irena found a job at the Emergency Room of the Regional Hospital. She saw quite a few deaths of her patients. Only after reading the book by Kalinovsky about life after death, which impressed Sergei so much, was she able to take it a little bit easier.

Irena remembers,
Sometimes I felt like I could almost see the soul leaving the dead body. For many I was their last companion, so people shared with me their last thoughts and repented their sins. I was not yet mature in my faith, but even so I always listened to them and tried to bring them peace. I told them that death was not the end but rather a crossover to another life which was going to be even better. I told them the names of great scientists who believed in life after death—Einstein, Pavlov, Pasteur—and also famous writers such as Dostoevsky, Tolstoy, and Solzhenitsyn. Some of the patients seemed very comforted.

Soon the couple felt that the knowledge they received from the church and books was not enough. They wanted more serious religious training. They were very interested when somebody told them that there was an opportunity for them to enter the Riga Theological Interdenominational Seminary. Rick Renner, who was well known for his TV services, was teaching there at that time. So, Sergei and Irena left their home in Voronezh and went to Riga, Latvia. They took the entrance exams, but did not receive scores high enough to enter. However, the seminary administration heard about this sincere young couple looking for their true calling. Later, the Kovrigins learned that the seminary president himself prayed about their case and the Lord told him to accept them into the seminary.

With God's help the young couple began their training. After graduation, the Kovrigins worked for a charismatic church. They went as missionaries to the city of Cherepovets, where they stayed for two years. Sergei was working as the pastor's assistant and Irena as Director of the Children's program.

When the Cherepovets mission was over, they returned to their home city of Voronezh. There they met the Methodists and pastor Vyacheslav Kim. They began to attend his church. The teachings of John Wesley and the outreach missions of the church seemed to be very close to the couple's beliefs. Soon, they could not imagine their future without the Methodist church.

By then they had two children, Masha and Daniel. Irena and Sergei asked the Lord to give them another child. Even before it was conceived, they promised that child to the Lord. And God heard them. Irena was pregnant when the Lord challenged her with a trial. The future mother had a very bad case of preeclampsia. On her fifteenth week of pregnancy, the doctors declared, "Have an abortion or face death." Sergei started to pray.

Irena was firm, "Never! A child from God, to be killed? No!" But within the next three days, her condition was getting worse and the doctors were going to abort without asking her consent. They needed to save her life. Sergei was praying all the time, asking for the Lord's help. And his prayers helped! On the fourth day, Irena was able to stand up on her own. The crisis had passed. The doctors were very surprised, but Irena knew that it was prayer that helped. Ever since that day, everything went well and a little girl who was named Liza was born on her due date.

In 1999 she turned three years old. For the first two years of her life the Kovriginy family had been serving at the *Martha and*

Mary RUMC in St. Petersburg, where they had been sent by the Bishop.

"I cannot find any meaning of my earthly life other than to live for God. I devote Him everything I am, everything I think and do. It is my reason for life, and I am very happy," Sergei says. "My prayer and my wish is that everything that the Lord has given me, all my abilities, are directed towards His service."

Irena sees her life meaning in the service of God as well.

"I can only repeat Sergei's words. There is no life for me without God. *God is our refuge and strength, an ever-present help in trouble* (Psalms 46:1)."

Nadezhda Nushtaeva

So the churches were strengthened in the faith
and grew daily in numbers.
Acts 16:5

"Nothing in this world happens by accident. Everything is predetermined by the Lord." Nadezhda Nushtaeva had never thought about that saying. She treated her meeting and acquaintance with Lydia Istomina at the St. Petersburg airport in 1991 as a pure accident. Lydia did not meet the stereotype of the priest. She was a modern, joyful woman, who liked to joke and laugh a lot. But at the same time she spoke about very serious things, such as God, church, and mercy. Lydia introduced herself as pastor of the *Ekaterinburg Methodist Church*. Before this, Nadezhda had never heard of a woman pastor. She was touched by Lydia's story about her ministry at the Ekaterinburg prisons.

Nadezhda did not know anything about Protestantism. While in college, she studied something about different religious denominations in her atheism class. But of course, it was all very negative. However, Nadezhda always accepted the existence of God, although she treated her relationship with Him as a very private matter.

With time, Nadezhda probably would have forgotten Lydia as we often forget our talks with airport strangers. But that woman was sent by God and therefore that meeting was not an accident. When Nadezhda returned to her native city of Ulyanovsk, she again met with Protestants.

An American group from Oklahoma came to Ulyanovsk to establish business and cultural connections. Lay people and pastors from St. Luke's United Methodist Church in Oklahoma City were a part of this group. The guests wished to learn more about Russian people and their daily lives and decided not to stay in the comfortable hotel "Venets" but with Russian families. That fact played a great role in the future development of the Methodist church in Ulyanovsk.

The American and Russian families became great friends instantly. Later, the American church sponsored a trip for their Russian friends to come and visit America. They were given an opportunity to see Oklahoma and visit different churches. After the Russians came back home, they decided to start a Methodist church in their city.

A Methodist pastor-missionary, Brian Kent, came with his family from the State of California. He began his work with Bible studies at his apartment. A cousin of Nadezhda's took her to one of those meetings. The charismatic Brian and his always-smiling wife Lorena made a good impression on Nadezhda. She enjoyed being there.

She remembers,

At our first meeting we formed a circle and Brian asked us to hold hands and to pray. He bowed his head, and so did we. And then I heard simple words, the words that we use talking to each other. Suddenly I realized that we are supposed to use such words when we address God. Thanksgiving was given to Him for gathering us together, for our joy of fellowship, and for God's love of people. The requests seemed to me to be rather unusual—that God would teach us and strengthen us in learning God's Word. Any Christian would not have noticed anything unusual, but to me everything was new and amazing. Especially, I liked the sincere relationships between people and the pastor.

Next time Brian asked everybody to tell something about themselves and several people told their story. Then the pastor passed around the Bibles and asked each of us to take turns reading verses from the Bible. Brian explained the difficult phrases and answered our questions. I was holding the Bible for the first time in my life.

With those Bible study meetings, Nadezhda's life began to change. She realized that there was a different kind of life, which had a great meaning. Nadezhda felt a deep desire to talk to others about that special meaning and the Laws of Moses. She wanted to hear and to read the Word of God.

For a year, Kent's family lived in Ulyanovsk. They held Bible Studies and children's meetings in their apartment and preached the Good News at local schools and universities. People of different occupations and paths of life came to those meetings—doctors and teachers, engineers and students, laborers and homemakers. They all wanted to know more about the Lord and to give Him their lives. Their number increased fast and soon the apartment became too small. Brian and the group found a bigger place which could accommodate over fifty people. Nadezhda tried not to miss the services and began to study the Bible and read Christian materials that the new church received from Moscow. She read the Bible every day.

After Brian and Lorena Kent left to go home, the new believers did not stop their meetings. They received great help from their sister church in America. Members of the church took turns preaching and praying every Sunday. Preachers from the United States came to visit and help with the church work every three or four months. In about a year another American pastor, Tom Hoffmann, and his family came to work in Ulyanovsk and train the local leaders.

When the local Government passed a new law forbidding the Protestant churches to use public places for their worship services, the Ulyanovsk church lost its place of worship. However, Tom was able to establish warm friendship with the other Protestant churches in the area, including the German Lutherans. As a result, Methodists were allowed to use the building of the Lutheran church for their meetings. The bigger and much nicer place, which was a real church building constructed at the turn of the nineteenth century and meticulously restored by the German builders, allowed the Methodists to broaden their ministries and to reach more local people.

Sometimes it is very hard for those who have lived without God all their lives to quickly change and confess their sins. However, the work with children shows its results much faster. Children are so much more open to the Word of God. Nadezhda pays them lots of loving attention.

One of the missions of the Ulyanovsk Methodists is the work at the local Retirement Home. They visit the elderly, bring them gifts, celebrate holidays and birthdays together and pray for each other. Seriously ill people are their special concern. Nadezhda and other church members' visits make those people think about their lives from a different perspective. They start learning about the Word of God. Many repent and accept Christ. *Blessed is the man whose sin the Lord will never count against him* (Romans 4:8).

Also the Ulyanovsk church started a Medical program. In 1998 a large group of doctors came to Ulyanovsk from the sister church in the U.S. They brought medications and were able to see many Russian patients.

Not long ago the sister church in California where Brian Kent was pastor which has been supporting the Ulyanovsk church was able to raise and send some financial help for a church building. It was not enough money for constructing their own building. But together with the Lutherans they constructed a facility which is called a Community House. Now, there are offices for both churches and rooms for the Bible Study classes and for choir rehearsals in that new building. In 1998 Nadezhda was appointed pastor of the *Ulyanovsk RUMC*. At the same time, the Bishop's office asked her to temporarily accept the responsibilities of Superintendent for the Volgo-Vyatsky District.

Nadezhda knows that there are no "coincidences" in our lives. That "accidental" acquaintance in St. Petersburg airport and a large group of new believers in Ulyanovsk had a deep connection.

We just did not know about it at first.

Igor Volovodov

Praise be to the Lord, to God our Savior,
who daily bears our burdens.
Psalms 68:19

All of his life, Igor has been working with people, first in the Institute and later at the factory. In the Electronics Division, he made his way up to supervisor. Laborers and bosses always loved him. He always got along with everybody although he had his own opinion as well.

His interpersonal skills let him quickly become a leader in the Voronezh *Church of the New Covenant.* Later, he became pastor of a new church in a different part of town. Again, his powers of persuasion served him well. He had always had a gift of being able to make people from all walks of life feel important, and his equal.

The fall of the Communist Regime, perestroika and economic chaos had made many people think about the meaning of life and reevaluate their priorities in life. First among these were religion and God. God alone could help and show people the way out of their difficult situations.

However, it is rare that the path to the Lord is straight and smooth. It was in these circumstances that Igor Volovodov went to the Orthodox Church to be baptized. He was looking for many answers which he never found there. He wanted to find the truth and to understand it, hearing from the Lord Himself. He found beautiful ancient ritual and elegantly-robed priests.

Igor remembers,

My sister-in-law and her daughter Natasha came to the Methodist church first. Natasha began attending the Bible School. One time I decided to go with her to see what she was doing there. I visited her class and then stayed for the worship service. I met normal people, not fanatics. They were true believers, about my age and social status. I enjoyed talking to them. The sermon touched me as well. However, I came there with a very skeptical attitude. So, even though my introduction to Methodism was very positive, my faith journey was long and gradual.

After visiting the church, Igor became interested in Protestantism, about which he knew hardly anything. So, he began reading philosophy books and a week later he went back to the Methodist church. He met the pastor. Vyacheslav Kim left him with a good impression and could answer many of his questions about the meaning of a person's life. Pastor Kim invited Igor to attend the Bible Study and to read the Bible at home. He became a member of the *New Covenant Russia United Methodist Church* and started to read the Bible regularly.

After about six months, Igor realized that everybody in the church was trying to do something for others and was helping as much as possible. So, Igor decided that he would provide some financial aid. The second chapter from the Letter of James about faith and works especially touched Igor. The Apostle James wrote in his letter that faith united a person with Christ but faith could not be real without works. *In the same way, faith by itself, if it is not accompanied by action, is dead* (James 2:17).

By then he had left the factory and begun his own successful business. Pastor Kim welcomed his idea of supporting the church financially and helping with transportation and the laws, which Igor knew very well. So, he became very involved in church administration work. Noticing his skills and abilities, the church members soon elected Igor to be the head of the Administrative Council.

I was growing in my faith and began feeling some stability in my life. I stopped being afraid of the difficulties or the future. The Lord was always with me. I knew that he would support, accept, and understand me, even if I made a mistake. He loves me and lifts my spirit. I received a new light of joy and peace in my life and calming of my soul. Before, I dedicated myself to achieving short-term goals and to providing for the future. I was always worried about our well-being. Sometimes, I regretted leaving my peaceful jobs at the Institute or at the factory where I received a monthly salary. After I learned the teachings of Christ, I realized that I should not live in my past or dream and worry about the future but I should live for today with faith in God to provide for me. As Jesus said, *And do not set your heart on what you will eat or drink; do not worry about it. For the pagan world runs after all such things, and your Father knows that you need them. But seek His Kingdom, and these things will be given to you as well* (Luke 12:29-31). So now I am not dreaming about my future, but living every day, loving others, and having peace in my soul. Major changes have occurred in my life and I am always "here and now."

Trips to Zelenograd, Ekaterinburg and Moscow to attend the Seminars of the Russia United Methodist Church played a big role in Igor's spiritual growth. There he had a chance to meet people like himself, who had recently found the meaning of life in service to the Lord. He listened to the testimonies of others and found proof in the Bible. Bishop Minor has influenced Igor's faith journey a lot. His kindness, calmness, self-control, and his ability to respond to people's evil with patience and love impressed him. The Bishop is a true Christian. Meeting Valery Khae and Ludmila Garbuzova made a profound impression on him as well.

Igor entered the newly opened two-year Biblical Institute Program called "East-West" in Voronezh. After graduation, he became a part-time student at the Interdenominational Christian Theological Seminary.

I felt a natural need to share the Good News that I received in the church and studied in the Holy Scripture. I began inviting friends over and telling them about my path to the Lord. People became interested and we started to gather for a regular Bible Study at my home. Some were already members of Vyacheslav's church, others from my group began to attend as well. In time, the number of people coming to my home church increased, and we decided to start a new fellowship in our part of town. Vyacheslav's church is located quite some distance away.

I soon found that while it was not very difficult to be a leader in the church of an experienced pastor like Vyacheslav it was totally different becoming the pastor of a new church and being on my own. At first, I hesitated and talked to Vyacheslav a lot, although he had approved my idea of starting a new church in a distant district from the beginning.

Igor found himself at a crossroads. He had to decide whether to leave his business and dedicate himself fully to the service of God or keep serving the Lord as a local leader in Vyacheslav's church and continue to work in his private firm. Probably, Igor would have spent much more time doubting his decision and hesitating than he did if not for a business trip to the neighboring city of Belgorod.

The road was very icy and very difficult with lots of hills. It was half snowing, half raining, and the visibility was sometimes as low as thirty feet. Often we could see the remains of recent automobile accidents, and overturned trucks and cars along the road. Every time I stepped on the brakes the car would spin around.

I kept thinking to myself, "Why am I testing my good luck going on these endless business trips? Sooner or later, I am going to crash like the drivers of the cars lying by the side of the road. Neither God, myself nor my family want that to happen!" I prayed, "God! Help me! Help me make it home!"

Suddenly a large KAMAZ truck with a trailer began to spin in the oncoming lane. In a moment I was going to crash into it. I hit the brakes, and my car started spinning on the wet asphalt. The truck driver was doing everything possible to turn his truck but it was sliding right toward us. Another moment, and my car was pushed off the road and landed in the deep snow. I was fortunate to land in a good spot because another yard or so and we could have ended in a deep ravine. We could easily have been crushed by the truck. At that moment, I thanked God for saving our lives and gave Him a promise to serve Him for the rest of my days.

Igor kept his word. He left the business world and dedicated himself to the church. On May 16, 1997, another Methodist church was registered in Voronezh. It was called *Apostles Peter and Paul's RUMC*, and Igor Volovodov was appointed its pastor. Over time, they have rented different places—libraries and a factory health facility—for the worship services. From the first days, Igor began to work on many church programs for adults and children. The Children's Bible School was opened, and the Musical Praise Group was formed. Igor was able to involve the President of the Voronezh Federation of Tae Kwon Do in the work of the church.

So now that person helps with the teenagers' ministry and has training sessions for the church's youth.

Igor's wife, Marina, is a doctor and his first assistant. She works with handicapped people who have musculoskeletal disorders. With other members of the church, she sponsors children at the Day Care and refugees from ex-Soviet Republics. The church provides material help to the needy refugees and the elderly. They also set up a counseling center for alcohol and drug addicted people. Many ministries are done in cooperation with Vyacheslav Kim's church and the *Resurrection RUMC* where Irena Mitina is pastor.

Now, I have a full life as Christ promised us. I know why I live. I live to serve the Lord. I often say about myself... *I have learned to be content whatever the circumstances.... I can do everything through Him who gives me strength* (Philippians 4:11,13).

Ludmila Pyatikh

You may ask me for anything in my name,
and I will do it.
John 14:14

Ludmila knew from her childhood years that God existed, even though she did not talk to Him or pray to Him. She was a pupil in a Soviet school. Generations of Russians were taught during those years that God did not exist and that He was created by other humans to keep people in fear. Most thought it was true. However, even without God they lived in constant fear and obedience to the Communist authorities.

When Lyuda was a child her Grandmother used to take her to church. But Lyuda doesn't remember much about that. They had an old Bible in her family's possession. When she was younger, she used to look at the rare pictures in it. When she was older, she did not have any interest in it. Until age thirty she led a busy social life, parties, students' skits, theatre, concerts, etc.

If anybody talked about God, she never listened. She always thought that only older people needed God. How old? She did not know. And to tell the truth, she did not care, because she had so many other fun things to do with her friends. The Lord had given Lyuda many talents. She wrote poems and music, had a great voice and loved to participate in drama. She was so busy that she could not stop and think. Very rarely, in the evenings when she was all by herself, she felt the uncertainty about the future and disappointment in herself. But the new day always came, and her depression was gone. She had many new things to do.

Ludmila remembers,
> Often it happens that we think about God only when something bad happens in our life. Only then we start to pray and talk to God. There is even a Russian proverb about it, "Until lightning strikes, a Russian man won't cross himself."

Ludmila had to experience an illness of her five-year-old daughter to come closer to God. Her child had fever, cough, and stomach pain. It happened on Sunday, so when Ludmila called the doctor for a house visit he could not come right away. Her poor child was getting worse, and mother was helplessly pacing the room. The doctor would not show up. Then Ludmila thought about her last hope and began to pray to God. She stood next to the window, looked into the skies, and pleaded, "Lord, help! Tell me what is wrong with my daughter."

Ludmila remembers that scary day,
> My eyes were directed at the skies. I knew that God dwelled somewhere up there, and I prayed. Then something scary and unusual happened. I thought I would faint from fear. It seemed to me that the skies opened up and I heard the voice of God. He called me by my name. I heard the voice of God! The Lord told me that my daughter was experiencing an attack of appendicitis. When I came to myself, I remembered that my daughter was complaining of sharp pain in her stomach, pointing to the right side. My mother was there with us at that time. So I told her that my child had appendicitis.
> Mom did not believe me. She said, "Why do you think so? It is just a bad flu."
> "God's voice told me," I responded.
> "What do you mean the voice of God?"

I did not want to argue and hurried to call the ambulance. When it arrived, the doctor confirmed the diagnosis, acute appendicitis. They took the girl into the hospital and sent her to the Operating Room immediately. The surgeon asked me if I had only one child. When I nodded, not being able to speak, he said that they would do their best to save her.

The surgery was complicated and took very long. The appendix ruptured, causing development of peritonitis.

Ludmila learned later that if the surgery had been postponed for another hour she could have lost her child. But the surgery was successful and the girl recovered over the next fifteen days. Ludmila did not doubt the existence of God anymore. She believed that her prayer saved her child's life. Ludmila went to church and lit a candle to thank the Lord and the saints. She asked the priest to pray a thanksgiving prayer for her daughter's healing and continue to pray for her full recovery. Now, Ludmila knows that *everyone who calls on the name of the Lord will be saved* (Romans 10:13).

"How did I end up in the Methodist church?" They invited me to join the choir. My friend knew how much I loved to sing, so she invited me. Our choir was very professional. The church itself was only one year old; it was the beginning. I was overwhelmed by happiness. I was singing spiritual music and hymns and listening to the Word of God. Later, our pastors, Lydia Istomina and Olga Kotsuba asked me to become the Choir Director.

Ludmila was very enthusiastic in her new position, and the choir learned a very large repertoire, including Rachmaninov's *Liturgy*, Tchaikovsky, Orthodox religious music and Protestant hymns. Ludmila conducted the choir and played the piano. Foreign visitors loved the choir's music and the choir received an invitation to come to Finland to visit different churches with concerts.

As was the case with some other members of the church who knew the Holy Scripture and wanted to tell others about it, Ludmila has gone to the women's jail twice a week. It took her a while to get used to being in a cell for a few hours. A cell is a small room with twenty to forty prisoners.

Society has turned away from those people in prison. If God loves lost souls why would He create this world at all? Ludmila understands it and keeps coming back to the poor people. Nobody talks about prisoners' rights in Russian. Prisons are experiencing very hard times.

After her visits, Ludmila has to wash her clothes right away. The prisoners do not have very many chances to bathe or wash clothes. But dirty and smelly, they cannot wait for Ludmila's next visit.

Ludmila shared with us:

I told them about God, read the Bible and asked them to repent. Often, they tell me what is in their heart and open up the truth they cannot share with anyone else, even the investigator. I realized that they need me.

I was especially shocked by the conditions in which the new mothers with infants and pregnant women live. When it is time to have a baby they are escorted to the hospital and later put back in their cells. The infants stay with their mothers in special rooms which are shared by five women. They all looked so sick and malnourished. Only a few received additional food from gift packages from their families in Ekaterinburg. Elena Choudinova, who joined me later, and I began to bring food and clothes to those who did not have any family. We tried to help both with our words and with our actions.

They listen very attentively and ask many questions. I answer all of them as well as possible, tell them about the Lord, and teach them to pray.

How do they welcome us? Usually just fine even though we walk into the cells without any guards or escort. Sometimes it happens that some women are in a bad mood, and say something bad to us. But I try not to take it too personally and do not get offended.

Usually, we start with question-answer dialog, tell them that we are from the Methodist Church, and ask what they know about God. Often, we hear an aggressive answer, such as, "Where was your God if he let us end up here?" We use quotes from the Gospels, and the Books of the Prophets and explain that there must have been a reason. If God sent them to such a trial, he must have such a plan for them or such a punishment.

I usually do not ask them what they did or why they were put into prison. If they decide to, they tell me themselves and confess.

Ludmila tells them the words from the Bible, *Even though I walk through the valley of the shadow of death, I will fear no evil, for you are with me; your rod and your staff, they comfort me. You prepare the table before me in the presence of my enemies. You anoint my head with oil; my cup overflows* (Psalms 23:4,5). Most of the women think that they were wrongly accused. But it does happen that sometimes a woman spends a year or longer in jail and later the judge pronounces her innocent.

Ludmila continues:

What are they accused of? I can tell you. The young ones, to whom we try to give more attention, are put in jail for robbery, fights, gang crimes, and sometimes murder. I asked a seventeen-year-old girl, "Did you just go and kill him?"

She told me, "Yes, and I think it was a good deed. He was a drug dealer, and many suffered from him. I do not remember how I killed him, but I am not sorry for it."

I tried to talk to her in simple terms, "You are still alive, you just have to spend some years in prison, and then, come out and see the blue skies again. But he is dead, and he won't see anything anymore. Don't you feel sorry for him?" I could not see even a spark of pity in her eyes! So, I tried again, "Did it do any good for you that you killed him?" Nothing in response.

When I talk to the young ones, I hope that at least a tiny seed of faith and hope falls into their souls. Even if they would not change and would keep doing the wrong things, their adolescent souls should keep something pure.

The older women treat Ludmila and Elena's visits more seriously. They ask to have a Bible and other Christian books and want to learn more about the Christian life.

In order to help the prisoners, members of the church often have to call or visit the authorities, trying to improve the conditions in prison. Also they visit the families of the prisoners. Sometimes, prisoners take advantage of the church members who try to help. Once when a girl and her mother lied to Ludmila about a crime the girl had committed, Ludmila decided not to go back to the jail anymore. She thought that she had seen enough of suffering. Her work in the choir was taking long hours of her life as well. But after missing a few of the prison visits, she realized that she could not live without those meetings with lost souls. The Lord Himself had sent her to minister to them. She had to forget her own ego and her hurts and to forgive, because there are people behind the bars who desperately needed her help, both material and spiritual. The Word of God that she brings to others, she cannot refuse them that.

For a few years, Ludmila Pyatikh has been helping to save people's souls. Every time, when she exits the jail, she has the same thought on her mind, "I came out but they stayed behind. I can see the blue sky and breathe the fresh air. They have to wait for the decision about their future life." At home, she spends hours praying for those who have to stay behind the bars, waiting for trial. The trial of man and the trial of God.

Ludmila Kapitonova

Then Jesus cried out,
"When a man believes in me,
he does not believe in me only,
but in the one who sent me."
John 12:44

An old Bible bound in worn leather holds a special place in the home of Ludmila Kapitonova, a member of the *Samara RUMC*. However, it is not used much these days. For everyday reading Ludmila has another, a more recent version. The old Bible is a family relic which went through Stalin's prisons and labor camps. It belonged to Ludmila's uncle, Vladimir Vasilievich Petropavlovsky. He was a well-known priest in Samara before the Revolution.

Luda met her uncle when he was in his late seventies. Tall and handsome in his younger years, by then he seemed to be a small and naïve old man, worn by years and prisons. But if you started talking to him that old man seemed to be tall and proud, like a never-broken spiritual prophet-preacher. During her youth, Ludmila was fortunate to hear her uncle speak a few times about people's kindness and their sufferings, and love of others. She remembered his words all of her life. When her uncle spoke it seemed like a large wave of grace and kindness covered Ludmila and took her into a new unknown world. But when she went back home, she had to take care of her everyday problems. So she returned to her reality and forgot about that different world.

For a long time Ludmila did not know that Vladimir Vasilievich used to be a priest. Neither her parents nor he himself talked about it because having a priest for an uncle was not good for a young Pioneer. Her uncle was a great teacher of life. He had taken the Word of God to others in Stalin's prisons and labor camps, where anybody talking to God was severely punished. He was able to save his Bible through all the searches and interrogations for twenty years! Nobody knows exactly how many people he brought to God using that book. Father Vladimir left his Bible to the Kapitonov family. He knew that they were Communists, but he hoped that the time would come and that Ludmila who used to listen to his words so attentively would see God's light and accept Christ. He died in the early 1960's in the town of Novokuibyshevsk. Only when all the Samara Orthodox high priests came for his funeral ceremony did Ludmila and her parents realize how respected her uncle was and that he was such a high authority in the Church.

Ludmila entered the Polytechnic Institute and the busy student life began for her. After her uncle's death, she did go to the Petropavlovsky Cathedral where he served long ago. She lit the candles but did not even think about God. She went because she promised her uncle that she would do it. So, she did it for him. In the Institute, she was elected a Comsomol leader of her class. She always stayed very busy. After the undergraduate degree, she went on to the graduate school and worked on her dissertation.

Everything seemed to be going very well in her life but then bad things began happening to her. First her father became ill, then her mother as well. Then Ludmila herself was diagnosed with cancer. Only then the godless family remembered about God and the old leather-covered Bible. They began praying. Also, they remembered that both maternal grandfather and great-grandfather were priests in the Orthodox church and that the father's family was Christian as well.

Ludmila's paternal grandfather used to have a mill, but the Soviets claimed him to be rich and took his mill away. He was left on the streets. In spite of that his son, Ludmila's father, supported the new authorities and even joined the Communist party. However, in three years, the KGB learned about his family's past and expelled him from the party. During World War II, he worked in a military factory and helped to move the factory from besieged Stalingrad to Kuibyshev (now Samara) through the battlefields. He was injured. Towards the end of the war, he gained the trust of the Party authorities with his faithful service, and they restored him in the Party. His wife shared his views. But before his death Ludmila's father began to doubt whether it was right to live without God. He even had a vision that his daughter would become a believer.

Ludmila's illness was progressing and doctors did not have any doubts about her bad prognosis. They said that they were not able to do anything else for her. But the Lord was merciful. Ludmila had a vision. It was the very first vision in her life. She learned that there was a town, Yesk, in the Rostov Region and an old man lived there. He was supposed to help. So, Ludmila left everything and went to Yesk. The old man used herbs and prayers as his medicine. Ludmila began to pray and to drink the herb extracts. After a while, she was feeling much better. When she came back to Samara, she found a sick mother and a father who could not get up from his bed. Ludmila's brother had left his child in the care of his parents. So, Ludmila had three people to take care of. She was taking care of her ill parents, assuming the responsibility of a mother role for the boy and working at the Institute. She did not have any time left for her private life. The years passed very quickly—she was 35, 38, 40. . . .

Only after her parents' death did she finally find a man whom she loved and cared for. A few years of happiness with him passed very fast. But he returned to his first wife and left Ludmila. She was forty-one years old, alone and pregnant. She decided to have the child and raise him by herself. Her friends and coworkers were very supportive. While she was at the hospital having the baby she received almost two hundred cards and notes! The Lord did not leave her side! Without God's help, she would not have had the strength to go on after the death of her parents and her former lover's deceit.

But her trial did not end then. When her son Sasha was six year old, he was outside playing in the snow one day. Suddenly, a car stopped nearby, and a man jumped out of it. He hit the boy in the head with something heavy and tried to drag his unconscious body into the car. It was so fortunate that the neighbor kids saw the commotion and alerted the adults. Ludmila almost fainted when she saw her unconscious son. She called the ambulance and took him to the hospital. Sasha had a very bad concussion.

The Militia told Ludmila that she should thank God that her boy was saved. That same day about thirty kids were kidnapped in Samara. They all were about the same age as Sasha. Why? They did not know. One of the theories was that children were going to be taken to Middle Asia and sold as plantation slaves. Another theory was about selling children to people who were involved in illegal organ transplants. Thank God, the boy was alive and with his mother although his trauma kept bothering him for a long time afterwards.

As a distressed child goes to his mother and father for comfort, Ludmila felt a need to be closer to her Heavenly Father. She began going to the Orthodox Church to thank God for her son's salvation. One time after the service, she stayed and talked to an old woman in attendance. The woman said that her legs had been bothering her lately and she was not able to stand up for the Orthodox services. Next Sunday, she was going to go to a new Christian church where people were very nice and everybody was allowed to sit during the worship service. Ludmila became interested and went to the Methodist church. It was 1991. *Samara UMC* was still in process of being organized. The prayer meetings were being held at a different place each Sunday. When Ludmila came to their service for the first time, they were meeting in a beautiful auditorium of the local Music school. She liked the service, especially because there were no mandatory rituals about which the Bible did not teach. She had always been amazed by the fact that the Orthodox Church claimed to be founded on the Bible but had so many saints they worshipped. The Holy Scripture did not talk about them.

In the new church, pastor Vladislav reminded Ludmila of her uncle with his manners and words of the sermon. After the service, Vladislav asked Ludmila to help and sort the humanitarian aid that the church received and was getting ready to distribute among the members. Ludmila stayed and helped. She came to help the next day as well. She was very familiar with that type of work. For a few years, she had worked for the State Social Services where she distributed material help and visited the elderly and the ill. Now, she began doing it on behalf of the Methodist church. During each visit, she witnessed to people about the new church and her path to the Lord. She invited all of her friends to come to the worship services.

From the very first day, Ludmila enjoyed the relationship which pastor Vladislav had with the church's members. They could always ask him questions or even argue with him. Ludmila enrolled in the Bible school. Every Sunday, she learned new truths from the Bible which she had missed when she read the Holy Scripture by herself. She realized that the Lord entered her heart while she was in the Methodist church. She did not start anything without a prayer anymore.

Vladislav helped her to heal her son. During one of the services, he hugged the boy, put his hand on the boy's head and said a prayer. Then, he said to the congregation, "A bad person did something very evil; he almost killed the boy. Now, the boy suffers from terrible headaches. Let's all stand up and pray for his healing." The entire church, all one hundred and fifty people, got up and prayed. And the headaches stopped. The boy was healed. He became a member of the children's group in the Bible school and later joined the youth group. He writes poetry and takes very active part in all activities of the church.

Ludmila brought many of her friends and neighbors to the church. Many of them accepted Christ. The daughter of Ludmila's close friend Eugenia found her future husband in the church. They were married in the Methodist church by pastor Vladislav. With the pastor's blessing, they decided to enter the Moscow Theological Seminary. Today, Natasha and Eduard Botovy are pastors of the United Methodist church in Kaliningrad. They often write to Ludmila, thanking her.

Many of Ludmila's friends were attracted to the church by the beautiful music. Ludmila always loved to sing. Often, her friends and neighbors gather together at her summerhouse. While the food is cooking, they start singing. The neighbors listen and ask, "What are those beautiful songs you are singing?"

Today, Ludmila, one of the leaders of the *Samara RUMC*, lives with God and measures all of her life up to Him. She is a director of the program which provides social help to the ill and the elderly. She often speaks to others witnessing about Christ. Her favorite verses that she often quotes are from the Book of Isaiah, *Turn to me and be saved* (Isaiah 45:22) and *The grass withers and flowers fail, but the word of our God stands forever* (Isaiah 40:8).

Ludmila Kapitonova has a few versions of the Holy Scriptures that she uses. Among them is the small paperback Bible she takes to church and to her visits with the elderly. Another version, the large print Bible, is used for her everyday readings. And the third one, an old leather-bound Bible which was her uncle's gift, is a family relic and it is not used very often. Ludmila opens it only when she feels the strongest temptations. Sometimes, she hears the temptations of Satan, "You have so many things to do in your garden. Why are you going to church? How are you going to survive the winter? You could live without God one Sunday!" When it happens Ludmila starts to pray and then she takes out her ancient Bible and opens it up to any page. With the Word of God she receives the Holy Spirit. She feels the life of those righteous people and sinners, to whom her uncle, Father Vladimir, preached from that Bible.

Andrey Kim

Give me the understanding to learn your commands.
Psalms 119:73

"I found the Lord by accident, unlike many others who found God during some kind of hardship. And it took me more than one try to find Him. The Lord was calling me, but I did not understand it and doubted Him for a long time." That is how Andrey once described his path to God when he talked to his colleagues who had been with him on geological expeditions.

Since early childhood, Andrey dreamed about trips to deep taiga, about crossings of violent rivers in mountain gorges and about camping at night by huge fires. He grew up among the untouched nature of Sakhalin, the large island which is east of Mongolia, east of northeastern China — an island in the Sea of Okhotsk just north of Japan, almost as far east as one can go in Russia. Later, he studied at the Moscow Geological Institute and his dreams of childhood came true. As a student, he went all over Siberia in search of uranium and other radioactive metals. As a part of geological expeditions, he visited all the places he dreamed about. After graduation he found a job at the scientific institute called "Hydroproject." His work, which involved designing new Siberian hydroelectric stations, had a romantic side to it.

Andrey had many opportunities to go on business trips to new places, including those outside the country. But he married a Moscow girl and stayed in the Capital. They had a daughter and later a son came along. The romance of taiga was replaced by everyday city life with its problems and many activities. Soon, perestroika began in Russia. The socialist empire had fallen. Business contacts and connections were falling apart. People became free to criticize everything and everybody, but other than that it seemed to many Russians that nothing but destruction came out of the change.

We cannot deny that freedom of speech is one of the great privileges and achievements of human society. Even our world began with the Word. *In the beginning was the Word, and the Word was with God, and the Word was God* (John 1:1). But if the Lord with His Word was creating the world, Gorbachev's freedom of speech broke the way of life we had become used to.

During those days, God talked to Andrey a few times, showing him the way to salvation, but Andrey did not listen to God's voice. The change in him began with a Korean language course taught by the American missionary of Korean heritage, Cho Young Cheul. Embassy workers and students from Seoul and Korean businessmen helped Cheul to teach the classes. Andrey's parents had spoken Korean at home, and he remembered some words from childhood. But during the years of expeditions and his Moscow life without a Korean environment he forgot most of it. So, two days a week he devoted himself to a Korean language class and meetings with other Russians of Korean heritage.

He soon discovered that two days a week of fellowship with his new friends was not enough. They began to meet on Sundays as well, when Cheul held the services of his Methodist church. Andrey was interested in learning more about God from the very first visit to the church and soon he attended every Sunday service. He liked the church for its uniqueness.

As did many others, I came to the service not just to hear the Word of God and praise the Lord but to chat with my friends as well.

After a month and a half, pastor Cheul offered Andrey a job to be his personal interpreter, to meet and escort Korean guests and to help during the worship services. It was a very hard decision to make. Andrey would have to leave his Institute and expedition friends. At first, he had many doubts.

It took me a long time to come to a final decision. It is true that there are lots of geologists. But there are very few pastors, and God Himself chooses them. If God had chosen me, I did not know it at that time. But I still decided to work for Cheul. The financial side played its role as well. Salaries were down, prices were up, and I was getting very little money at the Institute. Even though the pastor's job promised four times as much as my starting salary at the Institute it was still a very small amount.

Almost seven hundred people often came to the worship services in Cheul's Methodist church. Along with Koreans, who spoke or were learning the language, some Russians came as well. They were drawn by the wonderful sermons of the pastor, which were simultaneously translated into Russian.
Pastor Cheul used lots of quotes from the Bible in his sermons. So to be able to make good translations of God's Word Andrey had to learn the Holy Scripture.

Our pastor noticed my spiritual growth and one day he told me, "You are going to be a pastor." Pastor Cheul's sermons, which influenced many, did not touch me as much for a long time. He spoke about doing good things, about being merciful and about the importance of faith. But much of that was already in my heart. Perhaps that was what Cheul noticed when he prophesied about my future pastorship. All the spiritual matters—love, conscience, brotherhood—were an integral part of the geologists' life. One cannot survive in taiga without them. Helping others and self-sacrifice are very common on taiga expeditions. The words of the sermons about it did not touch my heart because I already felt that it was the way life should be.

One of the turning points of Andrey's life was meeting another American of Korean heritage, Mr. Lee. He came to Moscow for a visit. As soon as he arrived at the Intourist Hotel, he put down his suitcase and left it to make a quick phone call. Mr. Lee forgot that Moscow was just as dangerous as Los Angeles. During the few short minutes while he made his call the suitcase was stolen, and Mr. Lee's visa, passport and other documents along with his video camcorder disappeared with it. Andrey spent the next two weeks visiting the embassies and other places trying to restore the documents of the unfortunate American. During that time, Andrey noticed for the first time that there is some strange Divine Power which helps people in helpless situations. Before all the important visits to the high-powered officials, Mr. Lee would pray and ask God for His help. And every visit went very smoothly.

Andrey remembers,
> Once Mr. Lee asked me, "Why would not you become a pastor?" I told him the whole truth about my doubts. My last argument was: "How am I going to feed my family and my children?" His answer was eye-opening for me: "There were many of God's servants who died on the cross, were beaten by stones or killed by wild animals, but I don't know of any who died from starvation. I cannot guarantee you wealth, but you would never go hungry. Serve the Lord, and He will bless you, you and your family." When I heard those words, something moved inside my heart. To tell you the truth, my questioning had been more like an excuse.

Andrey kept working for Cheul, interpreting his sermons. (Pastor Cheul said that was why he had never learned to speak Russian: Andrey was always there for him.) Andrey received Holy Baptism in his church. In time, the Russian-American-Korean Theological Seminary was opened in Moscow. Cheul, its director, made sure that Andrey attended. "Even if you are not going to enroll, you will be helping me there," he told Andrey.

But Andrey liked the studies. He had learned much about the Bible while preparing to translate Cheul's Sunday sermons. But he still had a lot to learn from taking the seminary classes. Later, Cheul organized a trip for a group of Moscow Koreans to their historic Motherland, South Korea. Andrey was invited to be a part of that group. Those two weeks enriched them spiritually and let them see the life and ministries of many Korean churches.

If Andrey had realized before that pastor's work was very hard, he confirmed it again during the trip. He thought to himself, "I would not be able to do it; it is beyond me." First service was at five o'clock in the morning, Sermons were held not only on Sundays, but also on Wednesdays and Fridays, often three times a day. The number of believers was so large that not even the biggest church building could hold all of them. Some pastors had to preach up to ten different sermons a week! Andrey became more certain that such a life was not for him. But God had a different plan.

Andrey made his final decision after meeting one of the first Methodists in Russia, Lydia Istomina. God gave Lydia a gift of persuasion and faith. She was able to share her own beliefs with many others. Many former atheists turned to God with Lydia's help. There were people among them who later became God's servants: Ludmila Gorbuzova, Nelly Mamonova, Olga Kotsuba, Nadezhda Nushtaeva, Ivan Kozlov, and others. Andrey had met Lydia in Norway in 1993, where they represented Russia at the Central European Conference of the United Methodist Church. It gathered to elect the Bishop for the Russia United Methodist Church. Cho Young Cheul was invited to come, but due to some church business, he was not able to attend. He sent Andrey in his place. Lydia Istomina was the only person there who spoke Russian, so Andrey had many conversations with her. They talked about God, the purpose for life and the service to God. Back in Moscow after those conversations Andrey told Cheul that he was ready to start a small Methodist church and a Bible Study group.

"You are ready now, aren't you?" Cheul asked. "Good! But why do you say, a small church? You should not limit yourself if you do God's work."

Together with Vera Schepak, another seminary student, Andrey started to look for a building for church meetings. Soon, they found a nice auditorium in the library of the Perovo area where Vera lived. They convinced the library workers to let them use it for worship services. Then they placed announcements about the new church at the library and on nearby streets. All they had left to do was wait and see if anybody would respond. They should not have worried! God brought many people who were hungry for God's Word. The first service went wonderfully. People prayed, sang hymns, listened to the sermon and even stayed after the service. They asked many questions about God, the new church and the difference between the Methodists and the Orthodox. They were curious and asked how such young people as Andrey and Vera came to God. Andrey could not sleep that night. He was so overwhelmed by joy.

But his first joy was replaced by worries: Would people come next time? And they did and brought many others longing for the Word of God. Starting in November 1993, Perovo church celebrates its birthday every second Sunday in the month of November.

Some people receive God in one grand experience. To me, He came a little bit at a time and opened in all His complex grace, especially after prayer. I can talk a lot about it. At first, I noticed it during the incident with Mr. Lee. Later during the illness of my son. Nobody could tell us what was wrong with him. He would wake up at night, screaming, with a high fever. He complained of aching bones. I prayed so zealously, even screamed. I asked for God's help, but God did not hear me.

They took their four-year-old Vitalik to many clinics and hospitals, but all in vain. Finally, Andrey's wife took him to a person who practiced non-traditional medicine who was able to ease the pain. But after some time the attacks returned. Andrey's wife went back to that person and he helped again. But the next attack was very severe and it happened when the healer was out of town. The child was having a very high fever; he was shaking and crying from pain. As before, Andrey prayed but the Lord did not hear.

And then, the child said to him, "Daddy! Let's pray together the Lord's Prayer, "Our Father." Vitalik was attending the Children's Bible School and had learned about the prayer there.

We held hands and started to pray, "Our Father, who art in Heaven . . . . " And then, my son's face changed and he smiled. The pain was going away. I was a little scared and shocked by what was happening. The child was getting better right in front of my eyes. It was a miracle! After I came back to my senses, I started to pray again, thanking God for answering our prayer. My dear boy got better and soon fell asleep. But my wife and I could not sleep. We were stunned by God's grace. During the night, Vitalik woke up again, prayed the Lord's Prayer and fell asleep. His strange attacks never returned.

Andrey learned from that experience that prayers do not reach God if a praying person is aggressive or irritated. One should be respectful toward the Lord, calm and peaceful.

Now we know that prayer does help. If the attack ever does return we will just pray for complete healing. God opened to me that *"the prayer offered in faith will make the sick person well: the Lord will raise him up. If he has sinned, he will be forgiven"* (James 5:15).

Later, Andrey would often preach about the role of prayer in the life of believers. For three years Andrey served as a pastor of Perovo church. He realized that his personal studies and knowledge received from pastor Cheul was not enough any more. To continue his theological education he went to study in the Seoul University of Theology in South Korea.

Many times prayer helped him during his studies, especially during his last year. While Andrey and his roommates were at worship service one Sunday morning, somebody broke into their dorm room and stole their notebook computers. Andrey felt absolutely helpless. There were just a few weeks left until his diploma presentation and he had all his work in his computer. So he decided to return home and come back in a year for another try. The dean of the school could only offer his compassion. The pastor of the church which Andrey attended, who was Cho Young Cheul's father, advised him to pray. And he did pray. The pastor shared Andrey's problem with his congregation, and the people responded. They collected enough money for a new computer! Was not it a great result of prayer?

Andrey was able to finish his studies and receive his diploma. He came back to Moscow with a degree of Master of Divinity. Soon, he was appointed to be a professor and Director of the Moscow Theological Seminary in Moscow.

Many years ago, when friends asked Andrey how he found God, he had answered, "By accident." Now, he knows that it was not an accident, but God's plan that He has for every one of us. God's plan for Andrey was to carry the Word of God to the people of Russia.

Tamara Turkina

For whoever finds me
finds life
and receives favor from the Lord.
Proverbs 8:35

When Tamara was invited to come look at her new place of work, she was totally astonished at how terrible the Children's Home #1 looked and how bad the conditions were. The level of poverty at which the children lived shocked her. Her first thought was to try and leave this wretched place as soon as possible and try to forget. But something inside her made her stay, told her that, maybe, she could somehow help these orphans.

Everything about the orphanage bothered her: the children were not taken care of and about a fourth of them were actually missing. The rooms were large and uncomfortable. There were long, dark corridors and bathrooms with leaking toilets and faucets.

It was the cold month of February, and the poor children were freezing under their thin blankets. The heating elements were barely warm. All night Tamara was walking from room to room, covering cold children with their blankets. She could not sleep because of the cold, but mostly from her own thoughts. Who was going to help these poor children if she left just as many others had done before her? They would see the poverty and get frustrated from an inability to change anything for the better. Her inner voice told her she had to be strong and stay longer.

Samara Children's Home #1 is one of many thousands of Homes which are operating throughout Russia. The children live there from age four until they are sixteen to eighteen and finish their secondary education—9 or 11 grades depending on their abilities. The more talented ones go to the universities, the others who are not as talented or who did not want to make any effort in high school enter technical or trade schools.

The orphanages were created during the Soviet Regime, and the children there are raised as atheists. That is why the life of children in the Samara Children's Home #1 changed so amazingly after Tamara Vasilievna Turkina came to work there as Director. All of her life she looked for the way to God but remained an atheist and even joined the Communist party. At her new job, however, she found the way to God and brought the children from her Home to the Lord as well.

Those days were not very happy in Tamara's personal life. God had sent her many trials. Her husband had died, her only son had been mobilized for service in the army. She had been left alone in her empty apartment. After long debates with herself, she decided to accept the position of Director of the Children's Home. She hoped that she would be able to busy herself and get lost in her new problems which she knew were going to be many.

Before coming to work in the orphanage, Tamara had worked as Principal at one of the best secondary schools in Samara. What is amazing is not that the local administration or the School District Board transferred her to the orphanage, but that the orphanage children had actually requested her transfer. The orphanage had a very bad reputation among the local population. They called it "a nest of underaged criminals" because those kids terrorized local children and stole anything in their view or reach. Tamara did not know that. She had worked with some of the Home children during summer work camps, because children from her school went there as well. These motherless children recognized her talent as a teacher, her ability to find a common language with "difficult" teenagers, her being strict but always fair. That is why when the previous Director of the Children's Home left the kids themselves contacted the School District Administration with the request for Tamara Turkina to be appointed as their Director.

The administration was very surprised by the unusual request. After long doubts, they decided to talk to Tamara Vasilievna. It would have been easy to find somebody for the Principal's position in her exemplary school, but it was going to be very hard to get a knowledgeable and loving person for the orphanage. "Turkina with her enthusiasm, strong will and love for kids would be the ideal candidate for the position," the administration people thought. "She would be able to put things in order and help us out in the worst school of the District."

Tamara remembers,

During the very first days after I was appointed Director, Vladislav Spektorov, pastor of the *Samara RUMC,* came to me and offered to teach children "The Lessons of Kindness," to study the Bible with them and to try and give moral and financial support. I agreed immediately. Although I was an atheist, I had many doubts and I was bothered by the fact that so many intelligent and smart people had a belief in God. My relationship with the church and pastor Vladislav slowly opened the truth: everything on Earth happens according to God's will. At first, I was protesting against the truth. But I always remembered that I was baptized as a child, so God was always with me, although I did not feel His presence. Then I realized that it was due to the will of God that I unexpectedly left the school where I had worked for so many years and came to work in the Children's Home. The Lord gave me this trial, sending me to these children in need of my care and love. He let me know that I was not to leave them without help.

There was a large industrial plant within a block from the Children's Home. Tamara decided to go there for help. Using her energetic and enthusiastic personality, she managed to make an appointment with the busy president whose name was T. Krainov. She didn't tell him what she needed for the kids. She didn't complain about how little money they were granted from the City budget, but simply talked him into coming to visit the orphans.

Tamara remembers,

> The president found some time and actually came! When he saw the conditions in which the children lived he was shocked even more than I was on my first visit. That day was a historic date for us all. The very next day the president had a meeting with all of the supervisors of the plant. He told them to come visit the orphanage and then report to him about what each of them could do for us. He said that next week their most important task would be taking care of our problems, because those children were their future as well. And the miracle happened! New plumbing and heating systems were installed. Nice new beds were bought to replace the old ones. Walls were erected to divide the big rooms for twelve into smaller and nicer rooms for four children each. New linens and blankets were delivered as well. They even bought two small TV sets for us which became "trophies" for those whose rooms were the cleanest during each week.

Tamara began to institute a variety of simple disciplines. It had been so long since they had had morning exercises that the children had forgotten when the last time had been. So she made them get up for calisthenics. They did not want to at first, but later got used to it and even started to like it, especially when Tamara herself led them.

Part of her job included being Principal of the local school in the village where the Children's Home was located. So she began talking with the parents of the children who went to school with her orphans. They decided to take down the fence which had separated the Home from the surrounding houses and let children visit their friends. Both groups of children started to enjoy after-school activities together.

The kids used to get into the storage rooms of the local people and steal their canned goods. They kept doing it even after Tamara became the orphanage Director. In addition to having them apologize before local owners of the stolen goods, Tamara thought of another punishment. She withheld from the thieves' meals the amount of sugar which was used in stolen jam, for instance. The thieves had to drink tea or cocoa without sugar for a few days. Everybody knew about it, so the punishment was very effective.

Before the holidays, sausages and caviar and other delicacies were sometimes brought to the orphanage kitchen. Some of the children stole them. When it had happened before, the Director would usually write a special request for replacement of the delicacies. Most of the time this was granted. Tamara decided not to do it that way any longer. She told everybody that instead of having nice big holiday meals, they were going to have regular meals with smaller portions. The next day the thieves came forward with apologies.

With each day, Tamara's relationship with the kids was growing stronger. They accepted Tamara because with her their living conditions and the moral atmosphere had changed for the better.

There are a few other explanations why happy changes happened to the oldest orphanage in Samara with Tamara's coming there. One of these was the program instituted by a group in England in 1992 to bring orphans to the U.K. for study. Another was the visit to the U.S. by several children from Samara, including some from the Children's Home, who were invited for study at about the same time.

These two programs were important, but the most important was "The Lessons of Kindness" which took place at the Children's Home. A lady named Irena from *Samara RUMC* began coming there on Saturdays or Sundays and studying the Holy Bible with the orphans. The children were given their own Bibles. Irena showed animated films of the Bible stories to the youngest ones, and then they, together with the teacher, would put on puppet shows with the Bible characters. So, kids began their journey to God. They discovered that God loves them and they just needed to open their hearts for Him. The life of the orphanage drastically changed. God was with them. No matter what the kids did or what new methods their teachers tried, everything seemed to work.

Children were changing in front of Tamara's eyes. Of course, mischief still took place sometimes or even theft but the guilty were accused by their own peers. God's blessing was upon them.

In the summer of 1999, Samara Children's Home #1 was welcoming home its children who came back from America. For over a month, Gerra Knyazev, Slava Kostyunin and Dima Ponomariev had worked in a Bible Camp in the State of Ohio. The Russian children had performed their duties as caregivers very well. Americans liked the Russians so much that they invited them to come and work at the camp again in the summer of 2001.

Sometime ago a group of American volunteers, led by Martha Brice from the West Ohio Conference of the United Methodist Church in the U.S., came to help with the construction of the building for the *Samara RUMC*. The Lord's arrangement for them was to stay in one of the orphanage buildings, the usual occupants of which were gone to a summer camp on the Volga shore. The volunteers' help temporarily was not needed at the construction site, so they decided to help in remodeling the orphanage buildings. After work, they went to see the kids at the camp and quickly made lots of new friends. They learned about their lives and needs. The Director, Tamara Vasilievna, told the guests about each child's situation and how children in Orthodox Russia had become

Protestants. Martha Brice invited a few older kids who spoke English to come and work in the Children's Bible camp in America. Ms. Brice and the volunteers from Ohio have served at the orphanage every year since 1997.

From the very first days, the Orphanage Program was on the top of the priority list of the *Samara RUMC*. It was started with the birth of the church. God's will was for the church and the Children's Home to meet. The church's pastor was looking for people in need.

Tamara remembers,

All these years I have been living with the orphanage. If it had not been for the church, I do not know how I would have survived. Pastor Vladislav helped with everything. Although he was younger than I was, he had given me a lot, primarily the energy and skills of communicating with different people. He had an ability to enter the room and looking in kids' eyes, know what words they needed the most. And they listened to him very attentively. I was always so surprised that kids would sit still for an hour, listening and not talking to each other. In his sermons, Vladislav often talked about drugs and alcohol problems, trying to persuade children not to use them as did many of their parents. About 99% of our "orphans" are children with living parents, children of alcoholics or drug addicts who lost parents' rights or were put into prison. There are very few real orphans in the Children's Home. It has been much easier to work with the real orphans because they did not go through their families' hell. Those with living parents are the ones who needed the pastor's words the most. Vladislav used to come once a week. As did Sister Irena with her "Lessons of Kindness."

Soon, those weekly visits were not enough for our spiritual relationship with the Lord. Our teachers began taking the kids to the worship services in Samara. So many children wanted to go that our bus could barely carry them all. Meeting adult church members helped kids to come closer to God. Often, girls would bake cookies and bring them to church to share and to exchange recipes with women. Boys would give their handmade gifts.

At the end of 1997, Vladislav left to study in America. Olga Ganina, who replaced him as pastor, now comes to the orphanage. The traditions started by Vladislav are alive. The church began to help a detoxication facility for recovering drug and alcohol addicts near Samara, and sometimes took orphanage kids to meet with them, because the teachers were afraid that some of the kids had become interested in drugs.

The church helped children from the orphanage to find friends in England, Germany and America. Methodists from Samara's sister-city in Germany, Stuttgart, came to see the Children's Home while visiting *Samara RUMC*. When they learned about their needs, they sent them dentists equipment, new clothing and shoes, and toys for the youngsters. Now, Russian kids correspond with their German friends. The Director and the teacher of foreign languages for the orphanage were invited to visit Germany and participate in the exchange of experience and ideas with their German colleagues.

When Samara became sister city to the American city of Cincinnati, many American brothers and sisters from Ohio came to visit. Every time American groups visited Samara, they visited the Children's Home as well. They have decided not only to invite a few kids to the summer Bible camp, but to start a program similar to the British. Children would come for a year and live with families. Friends from Germany invited kids as well, but children do not speak any German yet.

Every visit of friends is like a celebration at the Children's Home. Guests always receive handmade gifts prepared by the children. The young artists give their paintings of the Volga shores;

others make crafts from fabric and paper, wood and metal. Others cross-stitch and knit their gifts.

"The harder my life is, the more support I receive from everybody," Tamara admits. "We thank all our brothers and sisters from the United Methodist church, the Anglican church, and other Christians for all their care for our orphans. Everything they do makes the children's lives a little better."

This is the story of the Samara Children's Home #1, of all their joys and problems. God's blessing helps them to live through sadness and elation, to live in hope and joy, as Christ told us. A former atheist and Communist, now a sister in Christ and Director of the Children's Home, Tamara helped to find that blessing of God. As Martha Brice wrote for this book, "Our teams from Ohio have received so much more than they could have given. We received joy and love from the children, extravagant hospitality from our Russian friends, and the example of one very fine, very strong Russian woman—Tamara Turkina."

Nataliya Chernova

Trust in the Lord and do good;
dwell in the land and enjoy safe pasture.
Psalms 37:3

A delegation from Morristown, New Jersey, in the United States, was coming to visit Kerch in the summer of 1992 as a part of the Russian-American program "Children of Peace." (Kerch is located in the southeastern part of Ukraine, on the peninsula between the Sea of Azov and the Black Sea.) It was going to be a historic event for this small provincial city, where they had not had any foreign visitors since the German occupation in World War II. The city had been closed to foreigners because of its shipbuilding and other military facilities located nearby. But with perestroika, all of the limits and borders fell.

The entire city prepared to meet the Americans. They tried to do their best to create an ideal itinerary for the guests. A group of young people led by Nataliya Chernova was going to escort them everywhere. That responsibility became a turning point for Nataliya. Her life was soon divided into life before, and life after, meeting the Americans.

Nataliya wrote in her diary,

> I was very fortunate to spend more time with the Americans than anyone else from Kerch. You can imagine our surprise when we learned that all thirty-six people in the group of travelers were members of the same Methodist church in

Morristown. They came not only to visit the city and its citizens, but to share the Good News about the Lord and Savior, Jesus Christ. They wanted to share it with those who had heard about Jesus but had never known him, and with those who had the Bible but had never read it, and with those who occasionally went to church but did not really know why.

Nataliya's mother professed to be a Christian and went to the Orthodox church on occasions. They had a Bible at home. Nataliya had tried to read it a few times. But it seemed too difficult to understand, so she put it aside. While she was escorting the Americans, Nataliya went to their prayer meetings and listened to their sermons. James White, the pastor from the First United Methodist Church in Morristown, especially impressed Nataliya. His sermon touched her heart. She was surprised that someone was able to speak about God with such simple and clear words. She began to wonder why she never tried harder to read the Holy Scripture.

The Americans quickly discovered that the people who came to their meetings had a great interest in God and even offered their help to start their own church in Kerch. Many people liked the idea. So they announced a meeting to talk about it. About seventy-five people came to the first meeting. They listened to James White's sermon and his story about his church and its future plans. The Russians found that brother Ilya Volokhov knew the Bible very well, so he was elected the leader of the future church.

Two weeks later the American guests left the city but members of the new group kept meeting for the Bible study and discussion. Nataliya's interest in God did not vanish, and she never missed a single meeting of the group. The Lord had a plan for Nataliya's life, she who had lived under God but did not know Him. Five or six years before, when she was a law school student, and later, when she was a successful lawyer in a respectable firm, Nataliya would not have imagined that she would one day repent and accept Christ as her Savior. To her surprise the Lord revealed Himself through American brothers and sisters and opened to the former Comsomol member and atheist the way to salvation and the eternal love of God.

Later, when she was invited to visit in Morristown she became assured that she had made the right first steps towards the Lord. Nataliya was impressed by American Methodist churches and the people. Having been an atheist and a non-believer in either the Lord or in the Communist ideas (many of which seemed to have been taken from Mosaic Law), Nataliya was impressed and surprised. She discovered that many of the people around her in Kerch and she, herself, were missing something in their lives.

Everything impressed me, the buildings, the people, and the simple relationship between pastor and congregation. All members were like real brothers and sisters to each other. I felt like I saw the Lord from a different perspective. It seemed like God Himself opened His arms for me. I realized that Jesus loved me despite the fact that I was sinful and unable to change myself. He loved me the way I was. Jesus told me that I had a future, and that was most important to me. This gave me hope and an inner drive, a stimulus to live my life. In a quiet moment I thought about Kerch. What a contrast! At the church where I had gone from time to time I felt miserable, unable to do anything, and very sinful. But with no remedy. I could not ask the Lord to forgive my sins, even if I bent down to the floor like the others. Then, in America, I realized *If we confess our sins, he is faithful and just and will forgive us our sins and purify us from all unrighteousness* (First John 1:9).

For about two years after that Ilya Volokhov continued to serve as pastor for the Kerch Methodist fellowship. Then it happened that he left for work in another city. By that time Nataliya had proved herself to be a true Christian who was ready to help any person in need. She could preach a sermon, she could conduct an evangelization meeting to attract new brothers and sisters to the church. Children who attended the Bible School fell in love with her. She possessed very good organizational skills. The Administrative Council of the church elected Nataliya their new leader.

So Bishop Minor appointed her to serve as a local pastor. Nataliya enthusiastically began her service by starting a number of new programs including the Program of Social Support to the needy, which is so characteristic of the Methodists. Together with her assistants from the church, she set up a free meal ministry for the poor and elderly. She began working in close cooperation with the Invalids' Fund on the program which was providing help to handicapped children. They distributed clothing, food items, and medications. A Medical Program was started in the church in order to help the sick and to prevent illness in healthy people.

For three years, Nataliya served as local pastor and by the time she was offered training at the seminary in Moscow, the church had over seventy adults and fifty children. Nataliya felt very satisfied and thanked the Lord for helping her find true calling in life, in the service of the Lord and His people. Still, when Bishop Minor offered her the opportunity to study further, she hesitated. She did understand that the knowledge she had received from study of the Holy Scripture, theological books, and pastor's training seminars was not enough for her to be a good pastor and preacher, and that she needed to study more. It was a huge dilemma. Going to Moscow meant leaving her elderly parents and a daughter who was to start first grade the next year. She would have to leave the prestigious firm where she had kept working part-time.

She hesitated for quite a few days until one day she heard the voice of God, "Go to Moscow and rely on the Lord." It is written, *May he give you the desire of your heart and make all your plans succeed* (Psalms 20:3).

I realized that the answer to my doubts was in the scriptures. If the Lord is sending me to the seminary and promising to help, I have to obey.

In 1996, Nataliya Chernova entered the Moscow Theological Seminary of the Russia United Methodist Church. The Lord helped with her family situation as He had promised. Her parents and daughter temporarily moved to Moscow. Nataliya found a part-time job to help provide for them. Thankful to God for His blessing, she enthusiastically started her classes and every day learned something new. The Lord led her on the way of finding His truth by opening to her new ideas, teaching with His Word, and strengthening in faith. At the Annual Conference of the Russia United Methodist Church in 1998, Nataliya was elected a member of the Administrative Council of the Russia United Methodist Church and a Secretary of the Conference.

From this time we have another entry from Nataliya's diary,

Now, I constantly feel the influence of the Lord. Every day and every hour, Jesus Christ is my life. When I compare my life into life without God and life with Him, I see that I have completely changed. I am sorry that I did not know Him until I turned twenty-seven and that I came to Him so late.

A Brief History
of Methodism in Russia
(1889 - 2000)

The motherland of Methodism was England, where John Wesley was born and began his preaching. "Finland was the door through which we entered Russia," Bishop William Burt, the general superintendent of the Methodist Episcopal Church in Europe, remembered in 1912 in the magazine *"Khristiansky Pobornik"* (St. Petersburg: 1912, Number 8, p.70).

However, the greatest role in spreading Methodism in Russia was played by the Methodist Episcopal Church of the United States in the nineteenth century and by its successor, The United Methodist Church, during the Methodist revival in Russia in the 1980s and 1990s.

The Swedish preacher Carl Lindberg came to St. Petersburg in 1881 to preach among the Swedish-speaking population. After three years, another Swedish preacher, B.A. Carlson, came to the capital of the Finnish Region of the Russian Empire, Gelsingfors (Helsinki). On November 7, 1884, the Methodist Church began its work there. Starting in May, 1889, B.A. Carlson went on mission trips to St. Petersburg on a monthly basis. He rented a hall, and on September 17, 1889, he preached the first sermon. After a month-and-a-half, the Methodist fellowship was started. On November 10, the pastor invited people for Holy Communion. That day was pronounced as the birthday of a local Methodist church in Russia.

In 1891, the Russian Government officially allowed Methodist Episcopal Church to work in all territories of the Empire. Methodism began to spread in the western parts of the Empire, which separated from Russia after the 1917 Revolution. Those were Kovensk Region (now Kaunas), Lithuania and Estonia, Poland and Finland. New churches were formed and buildings were built.

Missionaries from the United States, Germany and Sweden helped with the evangelization. In 1892, American Bishop Isaac W. Joyce started a fellowship in Vyborg (a small town near St. Petersburg on the Finnish-Russian border) and organized "Finnish and Petersburg's Mission." Although Methodist fellowships or "classes" already existed in Russia, they were not united under one organization and were not accepted as churches.

The 1905 February Revolution forced Tsar Nikolay II to give the country a Constitution. Among other things, it pronounced religious freedom. The same year brought a law about religious tolerance that allowed the religious minorities to exist.

The Methodist missionaries started their work among the Russian population in 1907 in Vyborg where the first fellowship of ten people was founded. On October 10, 1907, Dr. George A. Simons came to St. Petersburg as a missionary. He had finished the School of Theology at Drew University and from 1899 served as a Methodist Episcopal preacher in parishes of New York State. In 1907, he was appointed to St. Petersburg as a pastor of the Methodist Episcopal Church. With the help of interpreters, he preached in Swedish, Finnish, English and Russian languages. One of his interpreters into Russian was Hjalmar Salmi, who grew up in St. Petersburg. He had finished a Methodist school in Finland and became a preacher.

In the fall of 1908, an epidemic of cholera spread all across the south of Russia, finally reaching St. Petersburg. To help Russian doctors fight it, a group of Methodist Deaconess sisters came to the city and later formed the fellowship known as "Bethany." Their leader was Finnish-born Sister Anna Eklund. The sisters taught the Catechesis Classes for beginners and ministered to the poor.

Dr. Simons was very energetic about making the writings of the brothers Wesley and their followers available to Russian people. Due to his work *The Canonical Catechesis, The Doctrines and Discipline of the Methodist Episcopal Church,* a pamphlet *Methodists: Who They Are and What They Want,* and *The*

Character of a Methodist by John Wesley were all published in Russian. Then Dr. Simons started to work on publishing the magazine *Methodism in Russia* in the English language.

Inspired by the success of his publications, together with Hjalmar Salmi he began to print the Russian magazine called *Khristiansky Pobornik* which was a Russian variant of the well-known American Methodist magazine called *The Christian Advocate*. Salmi became its chief-editor. In the very first issue, the editors wrote: "Now, we are in Russia with its amazing history, unlimited possibilities and great future" (#1, 1909). In 1909 and 1910, the magazine published for the first time in Russia the sermons of John and Charles Wesley, in which the emphasis was put on the Reformation ideas, ways to salvation and personal acceptance of salvation in Christ.

In 1909 St. Petersburg's Methodist Episcopal Church was officially registered with the Russian Ministry of Justice, and at that time it united 132 people under the leadership of Dr. Simons, who was also appointed a superintendent of the Finnish and Russian Districts. Everyday, at the address in Vasilievsky Ostrov, prayer meetings were held in the Russian, Finnish, Estonian, Swedish, German, and English languages. This attracted different parts of the population. As *Khristiansky Pobornik* (#8, 1909) reported, thirty-three preachers, forty-five congregations with a total number of 1734 people were under the supervision of Superintendent Simons. Ten future preachers were studying at the Gelsingfors (Helsinki) Seminary in Finland; eight others went to study in the United States. Students were able to go to America because of the visit to St. Petersburg of the General Secretary of the Christian Student Council, American Methodist John R. Mott, in February of 1909. The possibilities of future missions in Russia attracted more and more American Christians.

In May of 1912, Dr. Simons took part in the General Conference of the Methodist Episcopal Church, which was held in Minneapolis, Minnesota. The attention of the delegates was brought to the "experiences full of miracles" from the East, as John Mott called the success of the Russian Methodist mission. The superintendent of the American Methodist Church in Europe, Bishop Burt, said: "There is no other nation in the world with such a great future as Russia. Soon, it will jump ahead for one or two hundred years and become the first in the religious, scientific and trade worlds. . . . We are there at the right time. Maybe we will be able to participate in the great future events" (*Khristiansky Pobornik*, #9, 1912, p.79).

In July of 1912, the dedication service of a new Prayer House was held in the village of Sigalovo in the St. Petersburg region. Bishop E. Nuelsen and other guests came and took part in the ceremony (*Khristiansky Pobornik*, #9, 1912, p.78). In the same year, the building for St. Petersburg church was bought on Vasilievsky Island, at the address of Bolshoi Prospekt, #58. In December of 1914, the Methodist Prayer House was opened there. The same building became headquarters for the Central Bureau of Russian Methodists, created by Dr. Simons, and the publishing office of the magazine *Khristiansky Pobornik* (*Khristiansky Pobornik*, #1, 1915, p.1).

With the beginning of World War One, most of the Western Russian regions were occupied by the German Army. Dr. Simons was not able to stay in contact with his congregations. The only one he had left was in St. Petersburg. Only Russian and English ethnic groups stayed within the congregation; they met on the Petrograd Side, Grebetskaya Street, #3.

During WWI the Methodists played an important role in the strengthening of Russian-American relations, which were of religious and humanitarian purposes. For example, the hospital in Kiev was opened with the cooperation of the Russian and American Red Cross organizations. With money from the American fellowship, a small military hospital was opened in St. Petersburg. It was sponsored by the American Ambassador to Russia, G. Merry. Americans gave an ambulance and founded a shelter for refugees from the occupied territories (*Khristiansky Pobornik*, #86, 1916, p.6).

Dr. Simons took a very active part in all of the projects. Representing the Methodist Church, he was a member of the American Red Cross Committee and a leader of the Committee of Petrograd Americans, which he himself had founded. He and other Americans working in Russia welcomed the February Revolution with great joy. The then current issue of *Khristiansky Pobornik* opened with the article "The Resurrection of Russia" which said: "The great Slavic people began their revival in all its greatness—from the darkness of despotic tyranny of medieval terrorism to the light of democratic freedom." (#102, 1917). On May 1, 1917, Dr. Simons organized a meeting in support of the temporary Government.

The number of Methodists in Russia was increasing very rapidly, especially after the great Russian writer Count Leo Tolstoy (1828-1910) published his ideas that each person should speak directly to God, not through mediators. If the October Revolution in 1917 had not happened, Russia would have had hundreds of churches where many thousands of Methodists would have worshiped the Lord.

However, the development of revolutionary events began to interfere with missionary activities of the Methodist Episcopal Church and many other Christian denominations. The ungodly times came. The "pogroms" were happening. Many Russian Orthodox priests were shot. Due to the departure from Russia of most leaders of Russian Methodism, the Methodist Episcopal Church in St. Petersburg stopped its work, and at the end of 1917 the publishing of the magazine *Khristiansky Pobornik* was stopped as well. Some time later it was resumed in the city of Riga in independent Latvia.

In 1918, Dr. Simons had to leave Russia. Sister Anna Eklund, the leader of the Bethany church, undertook leadership of the missionary and evangelization work. She tried to support the remaining Methodist communities, but the Revolution involved more and more groups of the population.

In 1921 Sister Eklund and Bishop John L. Nuelsen were able to contribute much to the outreach of Methodism by helping the starving population with both food and spiritual sustenance. With their help, the governmental publisher printed *The People's Bible* in Petrograd. In 1923, the Bishops' Board of the Methodist Episcopal Church helped the Russian Orthodox Church with a pledge of $50,000 dollars for the reopening of the Orthodox Academy, which had been closed by Bolsheviks earlier. However, the tension between the Government and priests in Russia kept increasing. The number of foreign missionaries was decreasing every year. In 1931, persecuted by Communists, Anna Eklund left Russia. The last Methodist church in Russia was closed.

The work did continue for a time in the Far East. Ten years before, Methodism had started to spread, mostly as a result of the ministry of American–Korean missionaries among ethnic Koreans. They worked mostly in Manchuria, in Beijing, and in Mukden—territories that never became part of the Soviet Union. In 1921, a building for the Methodist Episcopal Mission was opened in Vladivostok. On February 19, 1922, there were 80 churches with a total number of 3208 Methodist members in the Far East. But the same year the Communists took over Vladivostok, and the Soviets began to govern the whole region. The property and possessions of the Methodist Church were confiscated. Worship services were allowed to continue for a short time, but persecution had already begun and the future was evident. Missionaries from the United States went to China to work among Russian and Korean diaspora.

Uzhgorod United Methodist Church is one of the oldest Methodist churches in Ukraine. It began its work in the 1920's. (Western Ukraine belonged to Poland at that time.) When the Soviets took over, the church was closed. It reopened its doors with the beginning of Gorbachev's perestroika.

Methodism In Russia Since 1989

It was almost seventy years before the borders were opened again. When this finally happened in 1991 missionaries from different countries found ways to enter the country, including Methodists from the U.S.

The activity of this period is truly remarkable. What I have tried to do in this section is not to provide a comprehensive report but to introduce some of the early leaders, to show the eagerness of the Russians, the Americans, and the South Koreans to share the Good News, and to reveal, on a year-by-year basis, how God has blessed this work in Russia. It is important to note that almost every one of the churches I will mention is engaged not only in worship services, Bible teaching, and Christian fellowship, but is heavily involved in humanitarian assistance to its community in the name of Jesus Christ.

Russian Methodism—1989

In the summer of 1989 the Samara Methodist Church was established by two young Russians, Vladislav Spektorov and Anton Zakharchenko. They were friends, both graduates from the Samara Institute of Communications. Even though for some reason it could not be registered until 1991, it seems reasonable to say that the Samara church was the first Methodist church founded in Russia in the post-Soviet era.

Vladislav Spektorov had grown up in Samara, a large industrial city on the Volga River. He had spent many childhood summers on vacation with his family in Estonia. While he was there he had met and often visited with a Methodist pastor in Tallinn, Georg Lanberg. It was there in the Methodist Church that Spektorov had made his public confession of Jesus Christ and had begun preaching. Through Methodism, God touched Vladislav's heart and he felt called to start a Methodist church in his native city of Samara. His Institute colleague Anton was looking for a path to God and agreed to share Vladislav's work. In Samara they began meeting, using Wesley's model of the Holy Club. Together, they began their mission with Christian literature from the Methodist Church in Tallinn.

Russian Methodism—1990

In December of 1990 at the New York Annual Conference in the United States Bishop Dale White appointed Cho Young Cheul to be a missionary to Moscow. Members of the church in Moscow were at first South Korean businessmen, workers at diplomatic missions and Russians of Korean origin. The first service was on June 15 in the American-Korean UMC which had been pioneered by the South Korean diplomat Chang Son Kum. Korean-American missionary Dea Hee Kim preached the first sermon. The services were conducted in Korean and English, but later the synchronized translation into Russia was also offered. Cho Young Cheul served as the pastor of the first Methodist Church in Moscow and also organized and opened the Russian-American-Korean Seminary for Russians who had accepted Christ and wanted to become leaders of the new Methodist churches. Several of the current successful leaders of Moscow Methodist churches—Dmitry Lee. Valery Khae, Andrey Kim, Vyacheslav Kim—started as parishioners of his church.

Cho Young Cheul actively evangelized the Russian population, and not only from his pulpit. He opened classes in the Korean language for ethnic Koreans, many of whom had forgotten their native language during the years of Bolshevik genocide.

In July of 1990, the American pastor/missionary Rev. Dwight Ramsey began his work in Ekaterinburg. Lydia and Irina Istomina, Elena Stepanova, Olga Kotsuba, and others were present at the beginnings of the church. Together with Dwight Ramsey they started a Methodist Church that was registered in November of 1990.

In Moscow, the Korean-American missionary Yo Han Choi started the church named *The Way, The Truth, and the Life* in the early 1990's. This fellowship also became a school for many future leaders of the Russian Methodist movement—Nikolay Dalakyan, Fyodor Drozhzhin, Lev Mikhailov, Valery Patkevich and others began their spiritual revival and journey to the Lord at this church, and received wonderful training in ministry.

About that time another American, Bruce Englis, formed Methodist groups in St. Petersburg and Pushkin. He started several churches in a very short time. Russian people were hungry for God's Word and eagerly came to the evangelism meetings. From the many fellowships started by Englis, there were two, Bethany and Holy Trinity, which later chose to become affiliated with the Russia United Methodist Church. Others are now named "The Methodists of the Full Gospel" and lead an independent existence under the leadership of Elena Roukavishnikova. Some of the fellowships did not survive.

Russian Methodism—1991

In January, Bishop J. Woodrow Hearn, then president of the UM General Board of Global Ministries, and Dr. Randolph Nugent, General Secretary of that Board, met in Moscow with Russian Orthodox leaders. As Marilyn Oden says in her excellent book *Land of Sickles and Crosses*, they met "to build ecumenical bridges, to learn of missional needs and devise cooperative efforts for assistance."

Another Korean-American missionary, Yo Han Choi, came to Moscow and started helping with the new group of believers at *Moscow United Methodist Church*.

Bishop Hans Vaxby (Northern European Central Conference) and Bishop William B. Oden (Louisiana Conference) visited Ekaterinburg, and consecrated Lydia Istomina, the first Russian woman in the history of Methodism to become a Local Pastor. In September there began a strong relationship between the *First RUMC* of Ekaterinburg and the Broadmoor UMC in Shreveport, Louisiana, and the Louisiana Conference of the UMC in the United States.

The Sevastopol United Methodist Church was started by Lydia Istomina, Ivan Kozlov, and Dwight Ramsey.

In November, the Council of Bishops of the United Methodist Church appointed Bishop Ruediger Minor as Director of the Russia Initiative for Methodist development in Russia. He began to coordinate the work of the Moscow churches and groups in other Russian cities.

Bill and Grace Warnock moved to Moscow to work with Bishop Minor as Field Treasurer.

The Pskov RUMC was founded by Dwight Ramsey and Irina and Lydia Istomina from the *First RUMC* in Ekaterinburg.

Russian Methodism—1992

In January, Dwight Ramsey and the Istomina sisters started a church in St. Petersburg. They wrote its Ustav (Rules) and bathed it in prayer. In July, the Istomina sisters together with Andrey Pupko, Roman Tselner, and other believers gathered for a prayer meeting on the Twelfth Lane of the Vasilievsky Island, near the basement of the old (pre-revolutionary) Methodist church. They prayed and promised the Lord to dedicate their lives to the opening of new Russian Methodist churches. Also, they made a petition to the Government to return to them the buildings which belonged to the church before the Revolution. But the petition was ignored. Irina Istomina became the first leader of the *First United Methodist*

Church. Her assistants were Maria Volkova and Alexandra Bondarenko. On April 16 the church in Ekaterinburg had to re-register their church under a new name. The City Administration was going to tax the church for the use of the word "Russia" in their name. For this reason, The *First United Methodist Church of Russia* had to change its name to the *First United Methodist Church, Ekaterinburg, Russia.* By that time the First UMC in Ekaterinburg had its own newspaper "Svetoch" that was available to all other Methodist churches in Russia, and participated in the first Methodist Broadcast with the USA, "East Meets West" in Moscow. On April 21 the largest military airplane (Ruslan) landed in Ekaterinburg with the humanitarian aid from many American Methodist Churches that was collected by the Broadmoor UMC in Shreveport, Louisiana, in cooperation with the UMCOR (United Methodist Committee on Relief), and the members of the church began distributing food and medical supplies among low income families.

Bishop Reudiger Minor met in Moscow in August of 1992 with Methodists from congregations in the CIS and representatives from the U.S. to establish the Eurasian Annual Conference. This was the official re-launch of Russian Methodism. There were now four organized local Methodist churches in Russia (Moscow, Samara, Ekaterinburg) and several from other parts of the CIS.

It is truly amazing that people from two nations that had so recently been enemies could become partners in humanitarian and spiritual ministries. God was at work in the hearts of men and women through programs like The Russia Initiative. The Russia Initiative, led by Dr. Bruce Weaver, is a program developed by the General Board of Global Ministries, the Council of Bishops, and other General Agencies of the UMC and the newly formed Russia United Methodist Church. By 1994 four United Methodist groups from the United States (totaling 46 persons) were engaged in College and University Ministries in Mozhaysk, Saratov, and Oriskini. Nineteen U.S. groups (totaling 303 persons) from United Methodist

Volunteers in Mission came to Russia to engage in building projects and humanitarian projects in Orel, Saratov, Bykova, Pushkin, Moscow, Mozhaysk, Vladimir, and Ivanovo.

Thirty-two UM Churches from the U.S. participated in the Partner Church Program of the Russia Initiative to do humanitarian work and to assist churches or fellowships in Kirov, the Southern Urals, Satka, Vyksa, Serpukov, Mobeliv (Belarus), Minsk (Belarus), Belaya Tserkov (Ukraine), Krasnador, Kursk, Novgorod, Troitsk, Saratove, Tomsk (Siberia), Volgograd, Kerch (Ukraine), Smolensk, Yerevan, Moscow, Voronezh, Lytkarino, Dubna, Ramenskaye, Ulyanovsk, Dolgoprudney, Magadan, Orel, Vologda, Magnitagorsk, Novorossysk, Chelysabinsk, Stavrapol and Pyatigorsk.

Growth of the Russia United Methodist Church has been rapid. In the year 2000, at the Rakovo meeting of the Eurasian Annual Conference in July Bishop Minor appointed pastors to eighty-eight registered churches. Reports from the six district superintendents indicated that many other sites would be ready for pastors in 2001.

This brief history of Methodism in Russia, the churches and lives of their leaders that were gathered in this book witness to you, the reader, about the revival of Methodism in Russia in our days.

Boris Mikhailov